WHAT PEOPLE ARE SAYING ABOUT

WHO IS THIS JESUS?

Dan has a true heart for reaching every soul with the love of Christ, whether next door or on the other side of the world. He is a real-life example of what it means to fulfill the Great Commission.

—DR. WESS STAFFORD
PRESIDENT AND CEO, COMPASSION INTERNATIONAL; AND AUTHOR OF
TOO SMALL TO IGNORE: WHY CHILDREN ARE THE NEXT BIG THING

How refreshing—and challenging—to read an entire book completely focused on Jesus Christ! In Who Is This Jesus? *Dan Owens will inspire you to go beyond a mere knowledge about Jesus, to truly encountering Him—as your personal God, Teacher, and Savior (and that's just a start!). Owens writes with a passion; he's truly encountered Jesus Christ; and he's devoted his life to helping others—all across the globe—to discover the life-changing Person he's found.*

—ANN DUNAGAN
MISSIONARY AND COFOUNDER OF HARVEST MINISTRY

Dan Owens has a wonderful way of bringing Jesus Christ to life—making Him personal and relevant. He paints an amazing picture of the character and qualities of Jesus and challenges you out of your comfort zone with Christ's teachings. You'll be inspired to become a fully devoted follower of Christ instead of a lukewarm participant.

—SHERI A. MUELLER
COFOUNDER, GROWTHTRAC.COM, A CHRISTIAN MARRIAGE NONPROFIT
ORGANIZATION

Dan Owens has a unique way of bringing the lessons of Scripture to life that comes out in both his speaking and his writing. It has been a pleasure to have Dan speak at Spirit West Coast festivals through the years, and I applaud his vision for eternity and his desire to reach the world with the life-changing message of Jesus Christ.

—JON ROBBERSON
DIRECTOR, SPIRIT WEST COAST FESTIVALS

WHO IS THIS JESUS?

DANIEL OWENS

Victor®

The Bible Teacher's Teacher

COOK COMMUNICATIONS MINISTRIES
Colorado Springs, Colorado • Paris, Ontario
KINGSWAY COMMUNICATIONS LTD
Eastbourne, England

Victor® is an imprint of
Cook Communications Ministries, Colorado Springs, Colorado
80918
Cook Communications, Paris, Ontario
Kingsway Communications, Eastbourne, England

WHO IS THIS JESUS?
© 2007 by Daniel Owens

Published in association with the literary agency of Sanford
Communications, Inc., 6406 N.E. Pacific St., Portland, OR 97213.

All rights reserved. No part of this book may be reproduced without written permission, except for brief quotations in books and
critical reviews. For information, write Cook Communications
Ministries, 4050 Lee Vance View, Colorado Springs, CO 80918.

The Web addresses (URLs) recommended throughout this book
are solely offered as a resource to the reader. The citation of these
Web sites does not in any way imply an endorsement on the part
of the author or the publisher, nor does the author or publisher
vouch for their content for the life of this book.

Cover Photo: Jesus Burden iStock
Cover Design: Two Moore Designs/Ray Moore

First Printing, 2007
Printed in United States of America

1 2 3 4 5 6 7 8 9 10

All Scripture quotations, unless otherwise noted, are taken from
the *Holy Bible, New International Version®. NIV®.* Copyright © 1973,
1978, 1984 by International Bible Society. Used by permission of
Zondervan. All rights reserved. Scripture quotations marked MSG
are taken from *THE MESSAGE.* Copyright © by Eugene H.
Peterson 1993, 1994, 1995, 1996, 2000, 2001, 2002. Used by permission of NavPress Publishing Group; and NASB are taken from
the *New American Standard Bible,* © Copyright 1960, 1995 by The
Lockman Foundation. Used by permission. All italics in Scripture
have been added by the author for emphasis.

ISBN 978-0-7814-4188-9

LCCN 2006932642

This book is dedicated to

Luis Palau

*Twenty years ago you gave me the privilege of
working with you in evangelism. You once
said to me, "I will help open doors for you,
but you will have to walk through them." You
kept your word, and I am forever grateful. The
longer I am allowed by the Lord to "do the
work of an evangelist," the more I hold your
spiritual stamina in high regard.*

*Through the years, the gospel of John has held
a special place in your heart. Therefore, I dedi-
cate this book, based on the teachings of the
apostle John, to you. Thank you, Luis, for
your friendship, your faithfulness, and your
encouragement along the way.*

CONTENTS

Acknowledgments 9

Introduction 11

SECTION ONE: JESUS, OUR LORD

   1.   The Word. 19

   2.   The Light of the World 27

   3.   The Lamb of God 39

SECTION TWO: JESUS, OUR SAVIOR

   4.   The Teacher 55

   5.   The Son of God 67

   6.   The Bread of Life 77

SECTION THREE: JESUS, OUR SHEPHERD

   7.   The Gate for the Sheep 91

   8.   The Good Shepherd 101

SECTION FOUR: JESUS, OUR DIRECTION

9. The Way 115

10. The Truth............................. 125

11. The Life 137

SECTION FIVE: JESUS, OUR VINE

12. The True Vine 151

13. Remain in Me 163

14. Bear Fruit............................. 175

About the Author and Eternity Minded Ministries. . . . 187

Free Online Resources 189

Notes....................................... 190

ACKNOWLEDGMENTS

I want to express my thanks to Craig Bubeck, whose vision and encouragement have meant the world to me, and to the rest of the team at Cook Communications.

My deep thanks to Carl Dawson, my "Barnabas" as we've served together with Eternity Minded Ministries around the globe. Your loyalty, tireless efforts, and joy in the Lord have been an inspiration to me.

Thanks to Karen Weitzel for typing the first draft of my manuscript—never an easy task! My deep thanks to David Sanford, president of Sanford Communications, Inc., who helped turn my publishing dreams into a reality. As well, special thanks to SCI associate editors Elizabeth Jones and Rebekah Clark, who helped polish each chapter and added the application questions.

My prayer is that this book will bring a new understanding of Jesus to many thousands of readers for God's glory, honor, and praise.

INTRODUCTION

Some antagonists scoff, "If you trust Jesus as your Savior, it means you're just stepping out in blind faith." But those of us who have experienced the depth of a genuine relationship with Christ know that it's much more than a leap of blind faith.

My youngest son, Taylor, loves it when I take him to the swimming pool. He stands up on the side of the pool, and I tell him, "Hey, Taylor, jump into my arms." In order to jump into water that is much too deep for him to stand in, he has to have faith. But it's not blind faith—it's a faith that has been built on years of experience. Taylor knows that I love him and that I'm always there to protect him. So when I say, "Jump into my arms," he knows I will catch him.

The Bible teaches us we have to exercise our faith. We step out in faith and say, "Jesus, come into my life. I want you to forgive me of my sin. I want you to put me on the right path, and I want you to receive me when my life is over." But when we do that, it's not just blind faith. There is an astonishing amount of historical evidence that deals with who Jesus was and who Jesus is to this day.

As we look at the gospel of John, we find in John 20:30–31 the great summary statement, "Jesus did many other miraculous signs in the presence of his disciples, which are not recorded in this book. But these are written that you may believe that Jesus is the Christ, the Son of God, and that by believing you may have life in his name."

All that John wrote sprang from his desire to communicate the reality that Jesus is who he claims to be, that Jesus is God, and that in Jesus, through our relationship with him, there is eternal life.

Jesus had humble beginnings. The way he came to earth, the place he was born, even his hometown had no real greatness. But his life—more important, his death and resurrection—changed the course of human history.

I recently reread the following classic commentary on the life of Jesus known as "One Solitary Life."

> A child is born in an obscure village. He is brought up in another obscure village. He works in a carpenter shop until he is thirty, and then for three brief years is an itinerant preacher, proclaiming a message and living a life. He never writes a book. He never holds an office. He never raises an army. He never has a family of his own. He never owns a home. He never goes to college. He never travels two hundred miles from the place where he was born. He gathers a little group of friends about him and teaches them his way of life. While still a young man the tide of popular feeling turns against him. One denies him; another betrays him. He is turned over to his enemies. He goes through the mockery of a trial; he is nailed to a cross between two thieves, and when dead is laid in a borrowed grave by the kindness of a friend.
>
> Those are the facts of his human life. He rises from the dead. When we try to sum up his influence, all the armies that ever marched, all the parliaments that ever sat, all the kings that ever reigned are absolutely picayune in their influence on mankind compared with that of this one solitary life.[1]

Jesus is a historical figure. There are plenty of writings and historical works that prove Jesus' existence. In fact, there is more historical evidence of Jesus' being on earth than there is of Julius Caesar or Alexander the Great. Jesus was a real person. That is something no one can really dispute.

When we look at history and current events, we can see that Jesus' impact on our world and on our society is huge. One amazing consideration is that some of the writings about Jesus, even those penned by historians, were written soon after his death and resurrection—when the eyewitnesses were still alive. On the other hand, the first biographies about Alexander the Great weren't composed until nearly four hundred years after he died.

The Jewish historian Josephus (AD 37–100) wrote a great work entitled *Antiquities of the Jews*. Josephus was not well liked by the Jews because he sided with the Roman government. But he did record many important things about Jesus. He wrote, for instance,

> Now there was about this time Jesus, a wise man, if it be lawful to call him a man, for he was a doer of wonderful works, a teacher of such men as receive the truth with pleasure. He drew over to him both many of the Jews, and many of the Gentiles. He was the Christ; and when Pilate, at the suggestion of the principal men amongst us, had condemned him to the cross, those that loved him at the first did not forsake him, for he appeared to them alive again the third day, as the divine prophets had foretold these and ten thousand other wonderful things concerning him; and the tribe of Christians, so named from him, are not extinct to this day.[2]

Then there is the Roman historian Tacitus, who wrote in AD 115 how Nero used Christians as scapegoats for the fire that devastated Rome in AD 64. Tacitus explained,

> Nero fastened the guilt … on a class hated for their
> abominations, called Christians by the populace.
> Christus, from whom the name had its origin, suf-
> fered the extreme penalty during the reign of Tiberius
> at the hands of … Pontius Pilatus, and a most mis-
> chievous superstition, thus checked for the moment,
> again broke out not only in Judaea, the first source of
> the evil, but even in Rome.[3]

In AD 111, Pliny the Younger wrote this about Christians,

> They were in the habit of meeting on a certain fixed
> day before it was light, when they sang in alternate
> verses a hymn to Christ, as to a god, and bound
> themselves by a solemn oath, not to any wicked
> deeds, but never to commit any fraud, theft or adul-
> tery, never to falsify their word, nor deny a trust
> when they should be called upon to deliver it up;
> after which it was their custom to separate, and then
> reassemble to partake of food—but food of an ordi-
> nary and innocent kind.[4]

These historical accounts lead us to several conclusions. First, Jesus was a wise teacher. Second, Pontius Pilate, at the urging of Jewish leaders, really did execute Jesus on a cross. Third, Jesus established a faithful following of devoted people who worshipped him as God, maintained high ethical standards, and did not waver in their beliefs.

If someone were to say, "Oh, Jesus Christ didn't really exist," it would be clear he or she hasn't read too much history. Serious historians do not deny that Jesus Christ existed. He is a historical figure—and he changed history forever. So why did he come to earth? What was he doing here?

Who is this Jesus? That is the fundamental question. If Jesus really is God and Savior, then there are some issues to which we had better pay attention. If he is not God, however, we can then blow him off and say, "That's all right. We can live how we choose." But if we really believe that he is God, the Son of God, the Messiah, and the Savior, and that he came to save us from our sin, then the weight of responsibility on us greatly increases. We need to understand who Jesus is, how he wants us to respond to him, and what he wants us to do with our lives daily.

As we study the claims of Jesus, I want you to go beyond thinking of Jesus as an irrelevant and dead historical figure. I pray you will see him as currently active in your life and as your concerned, caring, and empathetic leader. My hope, as you read this book, is that you will *experience* Jesus Christ.

JESUS, OUR LORD

CHAPTER 1

THE WORD

*THE WORD WAS FIRST, THE WORD PRESENT TO GOD,
GOD PRESENT TO THE WORD. THE WORD WAS GOD,
IN READINESS FOR GOD FROM DAY ONE. EVERYTHING
WAS CREATED THROUGH HIM; NOTHING—NOT ONE THING!—
CAME INTO BEING WITHOUT HIM. WHAT CAME INTO
EXISTENCE WAS LIFE, AND THE LIFE WAS LIGHT TO
LIVE BY. THE LIFE-LIGHT BLAZED OUT OF THE
DARKNESS; THE DARKNESS COULDN'T PUT IT OUT.*

—JOHN 1:1–5 MSG

Every December my family likes to read the Christmas story. As we read from the gospel of Luke or Matthew, we envision baby Jesus, Mary and Joseph, shepherds, angels, and wise men.

Have you ever turned to the gospel of John to read the Christmas story? If we look at the first chapter of John, we can see "Christmas according to John." His account gives us a unique way to view Jesus' arrival in this world. We find there the first name of Jesus: the Word. John writes, "In the beginning was the Word, and the Word was with God, and the Word was God. He was with God in the beginning. Through him all things were made; without him nothing was made that has been made" (John 1:1–3).

Jesus Christ was preexistent. His life did not begin at his physical birth. John takes us back before Genesis 1:1, before creation, before God spoke the world into existence. He tells us that "through him all things were made." Jesus, the Son, was an integral part of creation. He was "with God," present at the very foundation of the world, yet a distinct person from God the Father.

Then in verse 14 we read, "The Word became flesh and made his dwelling among us. We have seen his glory, the glory of the One and Only, who came from the Father, full of grace and truth." The Christmas story, the story of Jesus' journey to earth, is summed up in these words: "The Word became flesh."

Jesus: The Eternal Word

One night while my wife, Deb, was at choir practice, my son Taylor and I decided to have a guys' night out. As we drove down to the sporting goods store, Taylor was pretty quiet. Then suddenly, Taylor broke the silence. "God was not born. No one made him. That's cool." I was amazed that my six-year-old son could already understand that God has always been here, that he is eternal, that he was never born, and that no one made him.

It's astounding to realize that God has always existed as the Father, the Son, and the Holy Spirit. The Trinity never had a beginning and will never have an end. John reflects on the eternal nature of Jesus the Word, who as part of the Trinity, existed in the beginning and has always been, but who took the form of a human in Jesus Christ. He came to the earth as the Messiah. But in eternity past—before time began—he was the Word.

I have tried various methods to help young people understand the concept of the Trinity. The analogy of water explains how water comes in three forms—liquid water, steam, and ice—but all three forms are the same thing: water. The egg analogy demonstrates how the egg has three parts—the shell, the yolk, and the white—but is all considered one egg. Although no analogy can adequately describe the mystery of God existing in three persons, a physical illustration can at least help us begin to visualize the concept.

John in his gospel goes to great lengths to communicate that Jesus is God. He stresses the divinity of Jesus, that Jesus has the same divine nature as God the Father.

When I was a young boy, my family never went to church. Every once in a while, though, my mom would talk about God. Several different times, I remember asking her, "Where did God come from? If God created us, then where did God come from?" My mom wasn't a Bible scholar. In fact, I had never even seen her open her Bible. But my mom said to me, "God wasn't born. He has always been here." As a kid, I would lie on my bed at night and just contemplate that thought. It gave me a splitting headache. "What do you mean God has always been here? Somebody had to create God. How can God always have been here? How can he be forever? How can there be a forever?" Even now, when I can't get to sleep at night, I reflect about deep things, and one of them is how God, Jesus (the Word), and the Spirit had no beginning. They are eternal. That, to me, is one of the greatest mysteries in the universe.

John says, "In the beginning was the Word." The existence of Jesus the Word extends back to the beginning, as far as we can imagine, and beyond. God wanted to communicate to us, and he did that though the Word, his Son Jesus Christ, so we could know how deeply he desires a relationship with us. The eternal Word took on limited human form in order to reach you and me!

Jesus: The Creative Word

Jesus was involved in creation. God was the Creator, but Jesus, the Word, was his agent. Romans 1:20 states, "For since the creation of the world God's invisible qualities—his eternal power and divine nature—have been clearly seen, being understood from what has been made, so that men are without excuse." Even nature reveals God's existence and power.

Paul writes that nothing could have existed without Jesus. "For by him all things were created: things in heaven and on earth, visible and invisible, whether thrones or powers or rulers or authorities; all things were created by him and for him. He is before all things, and in him all things hold together" (Col. 1:16–17).

I recently watched a special television program about the Orion Nebula. If you live in the Northern Hemisphere and look carefully at the winter sky, you'll see the constellation of Orion, "the hunter." Orion has a belt made out of three stars close together. Another three stars seem to hang down from that belt. They represent his sword. If you view those three stars through binoculars or a telescope, you'll notice that the middle one appears to be a little on the fuzzy side. The reason? It's a nebula— the Orion Nebula.

After watching this program, I logged onto the Internet and found a picture of the Orion Nebula. It awed and amazed me to realize I could see something that is two thousand light-years away from my own driveway. It must be huge!

The creation of those amazing stars is just one activity in which God was involved when he created our planet. And John says that the Word was *with* God. That means Jesus also was involved in creation.

Not only that, but our Savior is not some long-dead individual who lived two thousand years ago and who today doesn't have a clue what you or I may be going through. Hebrews 4:15 tells us Jesus was "tempted in every way, just as we are." This Savior knows you very well. This Savior is intimately acquainted with all of your ways. David describes this knowledge in Psalm 139:

O LORD, you have searched me
and you know me.
You know when I sit and when I rise;
you perceive my thoughts from afar.
You discern my going out and my lying down;
you are familiar with all my ways.
Before a word is on my tongue
you know it completely, O LORD....
For you created my inmost being;
you knit me together in my mother's womb.
(vv. 1–4, 13)

This Savior knows what causes you pain and what brings you joy. He knows the sorrow you're dealing with right now, and he knows your plans for tomorrow. He's not impersonal or uncaring—he wants to communicate with us, to share with us, to lead and guide us.

Jesus is the creative Word who created everything we see, and he wants to experience tender intimacy with his creation.

Jesus: The Incarnate Word

"The Word became flesh, and *dwelt among us*" (John 1:14 NASB). *Dwelt* actually means he "pitched his tent" among us. The Jewish culture understood clearly what that meant because in their history they had a portable, roving tabernacle that went with them and occupied the center of their camp. It was there that God manifested his presence. It was the place where the people sacrificed and worshipped. When Jesus came and pitched his tent among us, he brought that same divine presence right into the midst of the people.

Theologians will tell you that this is one of the great mysteries—something we still do not understand. They have written entire books about John 1:14, all by itself. For me, the great mystery is the thought that if God, who created human beings, took human form, then it makes perfect sense when Jesus tells us to be humble and to put the needs and interests of others before our own (Phil. 2:3–4). If Jesus, as Creator, could humble himself to become a baby with human limitations, shouldn't we likewise act and live with a sense of humility?

I once watched a CNN interview with Larry King. He, of course, has interviewed hundreds of people in his career, but this time the interviewer asked him, "If you could interview one person from history, who would you interview?"

Larry didn't hesitate. He said, "I would like to interview Jesus Christ, and I would like to ask him just one question: Were you indeed virgin born?"

The interviewer asked, "Why would you ask that question?"

Larry responded, saying, "The answer to that question would explain history for me." You see, an affirmative answer to his question means that life is more than just natural—it is supernatural. Life couldn't possibly be meaningless, then; it must have purpose. It means that history is not random like many people think it is, but planned. It means that the end of our mortal life is not really the end. Larry King understood the implications of his simple question.

Later in this first chapter of John, we find Andrew and Simon as they meet Jesus for the first time. The first question they have for him is, "Where are you staying?" (v. 38). They were talking to the Messiah, the Creator of the universe, and the first question they had was about his lodging! They could have asked something deep and theological, but they just wanted to know where Jesus lived. Jesus said, "Come and you will see," and he took them on an incredible journey showing them where he was from. God came and dwelt among us.

There is an organization in California called SETI, which stands for Search for Extraterrestrial Intelligence. They spend millions of dollars on telescopes and other devices and count-less hours in their attempt to find intelligent life elsewhere in the universe. Ironically, all this effort is poured into trying to communicate with someone out there, while the whole time God has been trying to communicate with *them*. He seeks to reveal himself to all of us through creation, through music and art, and through Jesus. If we would only listen!

Who is this Jesus? He is the Word who revealed to us God's plan for humanity. He has been, and still is, communicating to us through his creation and through his Word. He is the Word, the Word who became flesh in the form of a little baby. He died for our sins and then rose again to give us the hope of eternal life and a relationship with God our Father.

Thank you, Jesus, for being the eternal, creative, and incarnate Word, who existed before time began, but who chose to limit yourself in time and space in order to be our Savior. May we always be grateful that you came to dwell among us.

Application

1. "God, Jesus (the Word), and the Spirit had no beginning. They are eternal. That, to me, is one of the greatest mysteries in the universe." What does it mean to you to realize that "Jesus Christ is the same yesterday and today and forever" (Heb. 13:8)? How does it help you to trust him more?
2. "This Savior knows what causes you pain and what brings you joy. He knows the sorrow you're dealing with right now, and he knows your plans for tomorrow." How does the knowledge that Jesus is walking every step alongside you change the way you approach challenges and difficulties of life?
3. "For me, the great mystery is the thought that if God, who created human beings, took human form, then no wonder Jesus tells us to be humble and put the needs and interests of others before our

own." How often do you put others before yourself? What opportunities do you have to practice
humility?

4. "History is not random like many people think it
is, but planned. It means that the end of our mortal life is not really the end." How can you see
God's hand in the "history" of your own life? How
has he guided you to where you are today?

5. "God has been trying to communicate with *them*.
He seeks to reveal himself to all of us through creation, through music and art, and through Jesus."
In what ways has God communicated—or been
trying to communicate—to you today?

CHAPTER 2

THE LIGHT OF THE WORLD

THE LIFE-LIGHT WAS THE REAL THING: EVERY PERSON ENTERING LIFE HE BRINGS INTO LIGHT. HE WAS IN THE WORLD, THE WORLD WAS THERE THROUGH HIM, AND YET THE WORLD DIDN'T EVEN NOTICE. HE CAME TO HIS OWN PEOPLE, BUT THEY DIDN'T WANT HIM.

—JOHN 1:9–11 MSG

Flipping through channels late one night, I came across a short special on Las Vegas, the city of lights. If you've ever been to Las Vegas, you know the place is all about light, and at night it is fascinating to see the lights, the colors, the movement of the light.

The TV program described one of the most fascinating light features of Las Vegas—the sky beam at the top of the Luxor Hotel. The pyramid-shaped hotel rises 350 feet into the sky and is crowned by a giant light beam that shines directly upward. This light is so bright that it can be seen from an airplane 275 miles away. In fact, it can even be seen from outer space! Thirty-nine lamps give off seven thousand watts of light, and each bulb costs about $1,200.

The hotel had to make the beam shoot straight into the air because the Federal Aviation Administration (FAA) didn't want it to startle airplane pilots. They also must inform the FAA every time they turn the light on or off.

There is something about light that intrigues us. We love to look at Christmas lights adorning houses in the wintertime. Everyone enjoys the sparkle of the stars in the summer night sky. Light represents goodness, happiness, joy, and contentment. Darkness evokes feelings of fear, danger, and evil. We associate Jesus with light. The Devil is connected with darkness. Light is almost always seen positively.

Heaven will be full of the brightness of God's light. The Bible says God dwells in light, and whenever people have visions or encounters with God, there is usually some form of light, like a burning bush or pillar of fire.

In the beginning of his gospel, John describes Jesus in terms of light: "In him was life, and that life was the light of men. The light shines in the darkness, but the darkness has not understood it" (1:4–5). Then in chapter 8, verse 12, Jesus calls himself the "light of the world." Let's explore some of the lessons light teaches us.

Light Reveals God

Psalm 27:1 says, "The LORD is my light and my salvation—whom shall I fear?" Psalm 36:9 declares, "For with you is the fountain of life; in your light we see light." In Psalm 104:1–2 we read, "O LORD my God, you are very great; you are clothed with splendor and majesty. He wraps himself in light as with a garment." Then John wrote in 1 John 1:5, "This is the message we have heard from him and declare to you: God is light; in him there is no darkness at all." Why would John say that? Why would Jesus say, "I am the light of the world" (John 8:12)?

Whenever Jesus used the phrase "I am," the Jews knew exactly what he meant. It was the same word God used to describe himself in the Old Testament, and they understood that Jesus was claiming to be God. In fact, in John 8:58–59, when Jesus used the phrase "I am," the Jews picked up rocks and tried to stone him. It was a bold claim!

The word used here for *light* has a rich historical background. The Israelites observed an annual feast that lasted seven days and that they called the Feast of Tabernacles. It was a reminder of the time the Israelites wandered in the desert. It was not, however, a time of mourning or sadness. It was a time of great rejoicing. It also coincided with the harvest, so there was a lot of activity going on.

During this feast all the Israelites would leave their homes, and they would erect tents in a big circle to form something like a courtyard. The tents were a reminder of the way their forefathers had lived a long time ago. It was a reminder of God's protection.

In the midst of the courtyard, they would light big candelabras. Every home had a lamp, and at night they would move to the center of this courtyard where the big candelabras gave off incredible light. That light reminded them of the pillar of fire that God used to lead them through the desert—it reminded them that God was always there with them. It was a symbol of his presence.

Jesus appeared on the scene and claimed, "I am the light of the world." That statement created quite a stir among the Jews. Not only did he use God's special name, but he also claimed God's unique role as a protector and guide and to be the Messiah.

The world in which we live is dark. Of course, there are moments of great joy and happiness, and life can be fun. But in general, this is a dark world. It is dark because it is under the power of Satan and because of our own evil thoughts and devices. We move more deeply into spiritual darkness when we refuse to examine the evidence in the universe for God's existence and for who he is.

George Lucas, of *Star Wars* fame, did not invent the dark side. The dark side has been there ever since the Evil One had his beginning. It is in contrast to that dark side that Jesus said, "I have come to reveal to you what God is like in this darkness. In this dark world, I have come to show you what God is like and to answer your questions about God." We know what God is like because we see what Jesus was like.

Because Jesus came to reveal God to us, we can know the answers to the big questions: Where did we come from? Where are we going? Why are we here? Jesus came to show us the way, to answer the deepest questions of our hearts, and to point us to God. Jesus is the Light of the World. Has he revealed God to you? Jesus said the Father would reveal himself to those who walk with him (John 14:9–10, 21).

In your Christian life, in your Christian experience, has God revealed himself to you? Does he show you new things? When you're alone reading your Bible, or when you're driving in your car perhaps listening to worship music, and a certain thought hits you—that could be God showing you something new. When you come to a new spiritual understanding, when a light goes on in your mind—that may be God revealing himself to you. Not in some distant place, two thousand years ago, but right now, right here, God wants to show himself to you.

We sometimes make an encounter with God harder than it needs to be. *God wants to reveal himself to us.* He does not want to remain hidden behind some screen or cloud. God wants to draw you to himself. That is why it is so important that we spend time alone with God, meditate, and ask, "What do you want me to do? What do you want me to be?" Because in that darkness and in that time we spend with him, God will shed his light and expose things in our lives.

Do you ever get frustrated? Do you ever think, *Lord, where are you? You're not revealing yourself to me.* I find in my own life that such feelings of isolation from God are normally my own doing, not his. He wants to reveal himself to me, but I get too busy with my life to take the time to wait, pray, read, and meditate on God. God wants us to slow down long enough for him to reveal himself to us.

Light Exposes the Darkness

Jesus says in John 3:19, "This is the verdict." That's a pretty strong statement. He was saying, "This is the way it is." Jesus explained, "Light has come into the world, but men loved darkness instead of light because their deeds were evil. Everyone who does evil hates the light, and will not come into the light for fear that his deeds will be exposed. But whoever lives by the truth comes into the light, so that it may be seen plainly that what he has done has been done through God" (3:19–21).

In the Bible, light stands for the purity of God—the purity of the divine family composed of God the Father, Jesus the Son, and the Holy Spirit. When we look in the Bible, we see that God dwells in holy and pure light.

Jesus also explains that there are people who are not attracted to this light at all. You've met them. You've been around them. They may be people in your family. They may be neighbors. They may work with you. Whoever they are, the light doesn't attract them. In fact, it repels them. They don't want to get near it or anything else that speaks of God, righteousness, or goodness. They don't want any part of that because they love darkness. They love evil and sin, and they hate the light.

This passage tells us that God will expose every deed. He will reveal what we have done in darkness. It's an awesome realization that, as far as God is concerned, everything we do takes place in the light of day. We can hide nothing from him, not even our thoughts. Everything we do is totally exposed to the light. No excuses. No justifications. God knows it all.

One of the biggest challenges I have faced as a father is the question of which child hit the other one first. We've put a man on the moon, but no one can tell him a sure way to figure out the answer to "Who started it?" It's nearly always a mystery. But although the issue may be hidden from me, God knows every transgression, and he will expose the action. Not only will God expose the action, but he also will expose the motive behind the action and the thinking and emotions behind the motive. Nothing can be hidden from God. Sometimes that makes us feel very comfortable to know that, and other times it really bothers us.

When people become Christians and ask Jesus Christ to be their Savior, something unusual happens. Over a period of time, things they used to do start bugging them, and things they once thought were okay suddenly don't feel okay anymore. There takes place what I call a continual repentance. A person comes to the Lord and says, "Lord, forgive me. Come into my life and save me," and then for a period of time—and in many ways for a lifetime—that person must continually deal with the issue of turning from sin.

There's a great way a person can tell whether or not he or she is a child of God. How do you view the dark things—the sins—you commit? Do you live in a kind of peaceful coexistence with those things, or do they really bother you? Even if you are attracted to darker things, does the Spirit of God reveal to you the danger in those things? As children of God, we may feel an attraction to sin but sense that it's wrong and can destroy our lives. We know it instinctively. We begin to see inappropriate material on television, and we think to ourselves, *That's not right.* We just *know* it because the Spirit of God dwells in us, and the light that is in us reveals not only the darkness that is in our souls, but the darkness that is in our world. And when we fool ourselves into thinking we can enjoy a peaceful coexistence with sin, we're headed for trouble.

Gary, a former zookeeper, heard that a friend of his had acquired a young raccoon for a pet. She figured she'd take the raccoon home, nurture it, and make it the family pet. But Gary told her it wasn't a wise thing to do. He explained that when the raccoon reaches about two years old, it goes through a change that may cause it to attack for no reason. A thirty-pound raccoon has the fighting power of a one-hundred-pound dog.

The woman listened politely but still decided to take her new pet home. She said, "It'll be different for me." A few months later, she required plastic surgery to conceal the lacerations on her face after the raccoon attacked her for no apparent reason.

The light that shines into our lives when we come to know Christ keeps us from looking at the destructive nature of sin and saying, "Oh, it will be different for me. I can *manage* the sin in my life." We recognize the danger and say, "No, if God says this is what's going to happen, this is what's going to happen." When God says to avoid certain situations or behaviors, that is reason enough to stay away from them. His light in our lives exposes the darkness and makes us realize we can't avoid for long the consequences of sin.

Light Overcomes the Darkness

J. B. Phillips, in his wonderful paraphrase, *The New Testament in Modern English*, said it this way: "The light still shines in the darkness and the darkness has never put it out" (John 1:5). We followers of Jesus live in a dark, hostile world that tries to put out the light. But the world cannot extinguish it. His light is in you. It's in me. And the darkness will never overcome that light!

There are times when we go into despair. There are times when we struggle with depression. There are times when we ask ourselves, *What are we going to do?* But the darkness is not going to be victorious because we have the light of life in us, a light that gives direction and purpose. How dark and hopeless life must seem for people who don't have that light.

Helen Keller, an amazing woman who became blind and deaf as a child, wrote these words about people who live in darkness: "I have walked with people whose eyes are full of light but who see nothing in sea or sky, nothing in city streets, and nothing in books. It were far better to sail forever in the night of blindness with sense, and feeling, and mind, than to be content with the mere act of seeing."[1]

There are people who walk through life with their healthy eyes, yet they don't see. The light shines, but they don't see the life that is around them. It would be better to live in blindness yet be able to experience God's love and all the emotions that go along with that loving relationship than to be a person who has sight but does not know God.

One reason the Feast of Tabernacles was so important was that it reminded the Israelites of God's protection in the desert. They remembered that their ancestors had camped every night around a pillar of fire that gave them light. It was always light for them.

I heard a Christian say once that God never allows his children to be harmed. I can't go quite that far. Throughout history, Christians have been martyred for their faith, and followers of Jesus have suffered the same sickness, troubles, and problems as non-Christians. However, it is true that we have a special degree of protection. We believers are creatures of the light. You may have noticed that most of the violence in your area takes place after midnight and perhaps near a bar. Those who are not walking in the light are usually the ones who encounter the most troubles. One of the reasons we are protected is because as children of light we commit to obeying God's laws and avoiding sin. We benefit from the protection such a lifestyle provides.

One of the most gruesome murders I ever heard of happened to a college student from a Christian family who went off to college and became involved with some corrupt friends. One night the group went off to a place of darkness, and this student never returned. He should have known better, but he chose the darkness over the light. God provides light so we can avoid dark situations.

God also gives his children special protection in other ways—ways we probably won't even realize until we get to heaven. Then we will see all the times that God took care of us, prevented accidents, or kept us from harm. God protects us more than we will ever know.

A schoolteacher named Dodie was traveling through California when her truck broke down right on I-5 outside Sacramento. Her water pump had blown, and she had no idea what to do. As she watched the water pouring out of the truck, she prayed, "Please, God, send me an angel, and preferably one with mechanical experience." Not more than four minutes later, a big Harley pulled up, and a huge guy jumped off. Without even looking at Dodie, the man walked right over to the truck, opened the hood, and went to work.

After working for a while, he flagged down a fifty-six-foot rig and had the driver hook up a chain and pull the truck off to the side of the road. He worked just a little longer before slamming the hood and announcing, "It's all taken care of."

Dodie had been growing a little nervous after she read the words "Hell's Angels California" on the back of his black leather jacket, and she couldn't work up the courage to thank him. As the Harley man turned to leave, he said, "Don't judge a book by its cover. You may not know who you are talking to." He hopped on his Harley and sped away. Dodie still wonders if he was an angel, but from a different place than his jacket indicated.

It is thrilling to see how God watches over and protects his children. He is the Light that overcomes darkness. He keeps his children safe in his light.

We Need to Shine

Not only is Jesus *the* Light, but he asks us to shine, too. Jesus said to his disciples, "You are the light of the world. A city on a hill cannot be hidden. Neither do people light a lamp and put it under a bowl. Instead they put it on its stand, and it gives light to everyone in the house. In the same way, let your light shine before men, that they may see your good deeds and praise your Father in heaven" (Matt. 5:14–16).

Just as the brightness of the moon is a reflection of the sun, so our lives should be a reflection of our Savior, God's Son. We are to be for people a light in the darkness. Whatever our circumstance, whatever our situation, wherever we are, we need to be the light.

Sadly, many Christians shine rather dimly. I wonder if the reason most people do not share their faith is that they have little to share. They go to church on Sunday and have friends at church, but during the week, there is no light. They haven't allowed Jesus to fill every area of their lives. They can't be a light in the darkness because their little lights make little difference.

Many believers have become too much like the world. The number of divorces among Christians is comparable to those among nonbelievers; the way we spend our money indicates values and priorities that differ little from nonbelievers. Our entertainment choices often fail to give evidence of a mind bathed in God's light. The Light *has* come into the world. But it's up to us whether or not our lives will reflect that Light. It all boils down to choices and decisions.

If I don't have the Light in my life, I am missing out on what gives life meaning and purpose. If I don't reflect that Light, I must ask myself why. We need to examine our lives carefully and see if we even *want* to be light in the darkness and to be a light to the world. Jesus said, "I am the light of the world" (John 8:12), and calls us to be light to a world lost in darkness.

Lord, you shine into and within our lives. You illuminate. You bring understanding. You give us direction on the path of light. You protect us. You are the Light of the World. Help us to reflect your brightness as we shine Christ's love to this dark world.

Application

1. "That light reminded them of the pillar of fire that God used to lead them through the desert—it reminded them that God was always there with them. It was a symbol of his presence." What reminders do you have of God's presence in your life?

2. "When you're alone reading your Bible, or when you're driving in your car, perhaps listening to worship music, and a certain thought hits you—that could be God showing you something new. When you come to a new spiritual understanding, when a light goes on in your mind—that may be God revealing himself to you." How has God revealed himself to you lately? What have you done with what he has shown or taught you?

3. "God wants to reveal himself to me, but I get too busy with my life to take the time to wait, pray, read, and meditate on God. God wants us to slow down long enough for him to reveal himself to us." In what ways do you allow distractions to interfere with your time with the Lord?

4. "Jesus explains that there are people who are not attracted to this light at all. You've met them. You've been around them. They may be people in your family. They may be neighbors. They may

work with you." Who do you know who seems to be repelled by God's light? How can you reflect God's light in a way that may attract them to him?

5. "I wonder if the reason most people do not share their faith is that they have little to share. They go to church on Sunday and have friends at church, but during the week, there is no light. They haven't allowed Jesus to fill every area of their lives." Do you reflect Jesus' light to the world? What areas hinder you from shining brightly?

CHAPTER 3

THE LAMB OF GOD

JOHN SAW JESUS COMING TOWARD HIM AND YELLED
OUT, "HERE HE IS, GOD'S PASSOVER LAMB!
HE FORGIVES THE SINS OF THE WORLD!
THIS IS THE MAN I'VE BEEN TALKING ABOUT,
'THE ONE WHO COMES AFTER ME BUT IS REALLY AHEAD
OF ME.' I KNEW NOTHING ABOUT WHO HE WAS—ONLY
THIS: THAT MY TASK HAS BEEN TO GET ISRAEL
READY TO RECOGNIZE HIM AS THE GOD-REVEALER.

—JOHN 1:29–31 MSG

Shannon Wright was a teacher at Westside Middle School in Jonesboro, Arkansas. It was a typical day for Shannon. She had just begun teaching when she heard the fire alarm go off. She led her class out into the open area of the playground for this fire drill and immediately heard a popping sound. It was from a gun. She began to see her students dropping to the ground, bleeding and dying.

Shannon's eye caught a thirteen-year-old girl who was in the line of fire, and without thinking too much about it, she jumped in front of that girl at the same time that two rounds were fired. Shannon Wright died that day. She took the bullets and saved the life of that girl.

"Taking the bullet" is exactly what Jesus did for us. John the Baptist calls Jesus "the Lamb of God, who takes away the sin of the world" (John 1:29). John was a forerunner, preparing the way for the Lord. He was excited about Jesus. He wasn't just saying, "Hey, check this out." He was saying, "Look! Look! This is the Lamb of God, the one I've been telling you about. Look, here he is!"

His description of Jesus as a lamb brings up dozens of images from the Old Testament system of animal sacrifice. Let's take a closer look at a few aspects of Jesus' role as our sacrificial Lamb.

He Was a Willing Lamb

In both the Old Testament and the Gospels we see that Jesus came willingly, and he died willingly. However, John is the only writer to use the imagery of the lamb. What was he thinking about when he talked about the Lamb of God? What picture did John have in mind when he penned these words?

In the Old Testament times, lambs were used for sacrifices. John could have been referring to the Passover lamb, or he might have been thinking about the daily sacrifice in the morning and the evening. He also might have referred to what the Bible calls the "guilt offering" (see Lev. 5:14–15).

When I think about Jesus as the Lamb of God, I imagine Abraham as he got ready to sacrifice his son. Just as he was about to kill him, God stopped him and substituted another sacrifice in place of Isaac.

God also provided Jesus as a sacrifice for our sins. The "Lamb of God" conveys the idea that it was God himself who provided the Messiah, the Savior, the sacrifice for our sins.

In his book *The Case for Christ*, Lee Strobel writes about an interview with Dr. Gary Collins, a clinical psychologist, author, and a former chair of the Psychology Department at Trinity Evangelical Divinity School. Strobel interviewed him about the mental state of Jesus.

Lee Strobel first asked whether Dr. Collins, as a psychologist, believed that Jesus could have been insane. Collins replied, "Psychologists don't just look at what a person says. They'll go much deeper than that."[1] Collins listed several indicators of whether or not a person should be considered "crazy."

First, the psychologist looks at the emotional stability of the person. A disturbed person will frequently show inappropriate emotions like extreme anger or constant anxiety. "But look at Jesus: he never displayed inappropriate emotions," Collins said. When Jesus was angry, Collins noted, "He wasn't just irrationally ticked off because someone was annoying him; his was a righteous reaction against injustice and the blatant mistreatment of people."[2]

Deluded people also have misperceptions, Collins explained. They feel like people are out to get them. They "can't carry on a logical conversation, they'll jump to faulty conclusions, they're irrational. We don't see this in Jesus. He spoke clearly, powerfully, and eloquently. He was brilliant and had absolutely amazing insights into people."[3] Jesus understood people like no one on this earth understood them.

The third phenomenon Collins observed in mentally disturbed people is unsuitable behavior, such as wearing strange clothes or the inability to relate to others in a social setting. "Jesus' behavior was quite in line with what we would consider appropriate, and he had deep and abiding relationships with a wide variety of people from different walks of life," Collins said.[4]

At the end of the interview, Strobel asked, "What else do you observe about him?" Collins replied,

> He was loving but didn't let his compassion immobilize him; he didn't have a bloated ego, even though he was often surrounded by adoring crowds; he maintained balance despite an often demanding lifestyle; he always knew what he was doing and where he was going; he cared deeply about people, including women and children, who weren't seen as being important back then; he was able to accept people while not merely winking at their sin; he responded to individuals based on where they were at and what they uniquely needed.... All in all, I don't see signs that Jesus was suffering from any known mental illness.... He was much healthier than anyone else I know—including me![5]

Jesus, the Lamb of God, knowing he was the Messiah, knowing he was the Savior, came willingly to earth. He did so, not because he was crazy, but because of his great love for you and me. He willingly took the punishment, became the sacrifice, for us. He went to the cross with you in mind.

He Was the Sacrificial Lamb

Jesus knew and accepted the position of the sacrificial Lamb, the sacrifice for us all. "He himself bore our sins in his body on the tree, so that we might die to sins and live for righteousness; by his wounds you have been healed" (1 Peter 2:24). "For Christ died for sins once for all, the righteous for the unrighteous, to bring you to God" (1 Peter 3:18). "But you know that he appeared so that he might take away our sins" (1 John 3:5). He is and was the sacrificial Lamb who took away our sins.

It comes down to this: God is holy, and we are not. Therefore, we have a big problem. God is holy and just. His motives and thoughts are just. God acts in holiness, and we do just the opposite. How, then, do a holy God and sinful man somehow get back together? We long for that relationship with God, and God desires a relationship with us. So how in the world do we get there?

The theological word that provides the answer is the word *atonement*. Atonement means "to appease, to cover, to cancel." The key doctrine of Christianity is that Jesus died on the cross. He was the atoning sacrifice for everything you have ever done wrong, are doing wrong right now, and any wrong you will ever commit. Jesus paid that price and made that sacrifice for your sin and mine. That is why we sing "Worthy Is the Lamb," because he willingly became the sacrifice for us. It is as simple as John 3:16: "For God so loved the world." It's as complex as 1 Peter 2:24: "He himself bore our sins in his body." I don't understand it all, but that is the way God has chosen to bring us to himself.

Going back to Leviticus, we see that God prescribed different sacrifices and rituals that the Israelites had to perform in order to appease God's wrath *temporarily*. But they always looked forward to the day when Jesus would come and be the ultimate sacrifice—the sacrifice that would forever end the need for more sacrifices (Heb. 10:10; 1 Peter 3:18). "For the life of a creature is in the blood, and I have given it to you to make atonement for yourselves on the altar; it is the blood that makes atonement for one's life" (Lev. 17:11).

God chose blood. It is the most costly thing on this earth because when you give up your blood, you give up your life. Life is in the blood. And that is the way God chose to make atonement for our sin.

R. A. Torrey, a colleague and friend of D. L. Moody, wrote, "In the atoning death of His Son, instead of laying the punishment of guilty man upon an innocent third person, God took the shame and suffering due man upon Himself; and so far from that being unjust and cruel, it is amazing grace!"[6] And so it is. It's amazing that he would humble himself and come to earth as a baby, amazing that he, the God of the universe, would live the life of a peasant, and amazing that he would suffer humiliation and torture to pay the debt we owed.

In his wonderful book *Mere Christianity*, C. S. Lewis wrote this about the atonement: "We are told that Christ was killed for us, that his death has washed out our sins, and that by dying he disabled death itself.... Any theories we built up as how Christ's death did all this are, in my view, quite secondary."[7]

We can't understand it all. We must accept it by faith and receive the gift of the Lamb. John exclaimed as Jesus walked by, "Look, there he is! There is the Lamb of God who takes away the sin of the world!" I wonder if we really understand what that means and what he has done for us. Jesus willingly paid the ultimate sacrifice to bring us into a relationship with God. It was out of love that Jesus atoned for our sins. He could have chosen another way, but that is the way God chose—and he did it out of love for you and me.

We often compare ourselves with one another. It's hard not to. We compare our goodness to other people's goodness. Sometimes we go away feeling pretty good about ourselves. "Oh Lord, I'm not like that person over there."

We need to stop comparing ourselves to one another. We must choose instead to open the Bible and take a good look at the holiness of God and compare ourselves against him alone. We will then have a greater appreciation for the atoning work of Jesus Christ on the cross. None of us is good enough, smart enough, rich enough, or wise enough to make it to God. God knew there needed to be a sacrifice—a way to cover up, to appease, and to remove the guilt of our sin. His plan was to send his own Son, Jesus, to die on that cross for us.

I've traveled to India about twenty-five times since 1987. I have to confess that going to India is difficult—*foreign* to the extreme. Everything about it feels odd—from the interminably long plane ride to the uncomfortable trains.

During one of my more recent trips to India, in 2003, I was reflecting on how different it was from my first trip nearly two decades before. They recently passed a law intended to stop Christianity from spreading in their country. The ruling government wants India to be a Hindu-only country.

We ended up going to the state of Kerala. I had never been there, but it was reportedly the most Christianized state in all of India—its nickname is "God's Own Country." I figured it would be a safe place to go. We prayed, we talked, we planned, and we went to Kerala.

We landed in the capital city of Trivandrum. We knew prior to our arrival that there were some risks, and we had discussed various issues pertaining to our safety. We didn't know, however, that the legislature had recently held a meeting at which it had established a special police task force to stop us from preaching in Trivandrum.

When I heard that news, I told the guys who were with me, "If they put together a special police force on our account, I can guarantee you they will stop us." I didn't mean to have so little faith, but I realized that if you are wearing a bull's-eye, you are likely to become a target.

We knew that God was bigger than any opposition, so we got together and prayed. We worshipped. There were about ten of us in the room, and it was a great time of praising God together.

The next day—the day on which we were supposed to start—the police didn't even wait for us to get started. They came to the hotel, called a few of the guys downstairs, and ordered them to bring their passports. They didn't call me, so I thought, *Why go down? I'm not an idiot!*

The police said to my friends, "You're on a tourist visa. You can't preach here." After all our planning and preparation, they just shut several of us down. So we got together and had a meeting. The local coordinator was there, and he went around the room assessing the situation. "You can't preach, and you can't preach ... but, Dan, *you* can preach!"

Yeah, right, I thought. *Just because they didn't get me this morning doesn't mean they won't be waiting for me when I get up to preach.* But I agreed to preach that night.

It was interesting to preach for what may have been my last time in India. The crowd was smaller than usual because many had heard about all the police and didn't want to be around in case of trouble. Many of those who did attend came for no other reason than to see me carted off to jail! But two hundred people came forward to receive Jesus Christ. God is bigger than the opposition.

Nothing went wrong, and I went straight from the event to the airport and immediately headed home because my wife's mother had just passed away. On the way to the airport, the Indian who was with me, who was coordinating everything, got a call from the chief of police. The officer wanted to talk to him and wanted us all to get together. I was glad I was leaving. I wanted to miss that meeting!

As I flew home, I mourned at the thought of one billion people in India who might never have the opportunity to hear about the Lamb of God who takes away the sin of the world. Yes, there are churches in India. When evangelists come to speak at their gatherings, many people come out who wouldn't normally show up at church. But now the doors were closing.

We are talking about *one billion people.* Many of them still sacrifice to gods carved out of wood and stone. They are people who have no hope in life, who walk on the never-ending treadmill of reincarnation. As I boarded that plane, I actually began to cry as I thought about all those people who weren't going to have any evangelists come through their towns. If the most Christianized state in India shut down our evangelistic team, then what are all the other states going to do? Many of the other states have already stopped letting *anyone* preach. You can't get in those areas anymore.

Jesus died for all those people in India. They, along with others all around the world, need to hear that he is the Lamb, their ultimate sacrifice. I continue praying that someone, somehow, will get through to them.

He Is the Triumphant Lamb

Revelation 5:12–13 is a great song of praise to Jesus.

> Worthy is the Lamb, who was slain,
> to receive power and wealth and wisdom and
>   strength
> and honor and glory and praise! ...
> To him who sits on the throne and to the Lamb
> be praise and honor and glory and power,
> for ever and ever!

Jesus is the triumphant Lamb, not just in the future, when we will gather around his throne in heaven and sing to the Lamb of God, who is Jesus Christ, but also right now. He is the triumphant Lamb *today*.

As I sat on the airplane coming home from India, I reflected and praised the Lord for all the opportunities I'd had through the years to look into the faces of hundreds of thousands of people and see the change on their faces. I was scribbling out an outline for Eternity Minded Ministries for my next brochure, which I've titled *Changing Faces by Changing Hearts in Changing Times*.

I realized, as I have stood on platforms and watched people come forward—Europeans, Asians, Africans, and Americans—I have seen tears of repentance run down those faces. They become tears of joy as I observe with my own eyes the transformation of those people. That motivates me. When people ask, "Why do you go to India? Why don't you go someplace else?" I reply, "Because I've seen the faces. They're in my head, and I can't ever get rid of them. I don't ever want to get rid of them."

Changing faces—that's the work of the triumphant Lamb who changes the cold, hard, stony faces of people into faces of joy and happiness.

Brennan Manning, one of my favorite authors, tells the story of a man whose face was changed because his heart was changed by Jesus Christ. One of the man's friends, a skeptic, asked him a few questions soon after he accepted Christ.

> "So you have converted to Christ?"
> "Yes."
> "Then you must know a great deal about him. Tell me, what country was he born in?"
> "I don't know."
> "What was his age when he died?"
> "I don't know."
> "How many sermons did he preach?"
> "I don't know."
> "You certainly know very little for a man who claims to be a convert to Christ."
> "You are right. I am ashamed at how little I know about Him. But this much I know: Three years ago I was a drunkard. I was in debt. My family was falling to pieces; they dreaded the sight of me. But now I have given up drink. We are out of debt. Ours is a happy home. My children eagerly await my return home each evening. All this Christ has done for me. This much I know of Christ!"[8]

That is the triumphant Christ, who changes the heart and changes the face, the Lamb of God who takes away the sin of the world.

Timothy McCarthy was a guy who hated to lose when he was a defensive back at the University of Illinois. One day in

1981, he lost a game of a different kind. He and a colleague were flipping a coin to see who would take on an extra assignment on their day off from their jobs as Secret Service agents. He lost the coin toss and had to take the extra assignment, an assignment that changed his life forever.

On March 31, 1981, all the training McCarthy had undergone paid off in a split second. A shot rang out, and Timothy McCarthy, the Secret Service agent, instantly did what he had been trained to do. He positioned himself between President Reagan and the would-be assassin, John Hinckley.

You might remember the pictures splashed across the newspapers. McCarthy crouched in a football linebacker's defensive position, shielding the president. The second shot slammed into his stomach, dropping him to the ground.

Timothy McCarthy became a hero that day. He received awards and medals. Over fifty thousand get-well cards arrived at his hospital room, including one from the assassin's parents.

President Reagan wrote to McCarthy while he was recovering in the hospital. He wrote, "There will always be the special gratitude I feel for your extraordinary heroism on that one cold day in March. It is a gratitude words could never convey."

Timothy McCarthy took the bullet and left a man forever grateful, just as a mom and dad were forever grateful when Shannon Wright took the bullet for their thirteen-year-old daughter in Jonesboro.

Jesus "took the bullet" for us. He died in our place. It is even more amazing because we actually deserved to die. Undoubtedly, President Reagan didn't deserve to be shot by an assassin; neither did that little girl in Jonesboro. But we all deserved death for our sins.

Jesus paid our penalty, yet I wonder how grateful we really are that he did. Do we express appreciation and gratitude that Jesus, the Lamb of God, died for us willingly, sacrificially, and triumphantly? Are we really grateful? Or have we become so accustomed to hearing the story, to singing the songs—the old hymns of the faith about the Lamb—that they no longer stir our emotions? I ask God to keep me from ever getting to the point where I can sing the song "Worthy Is the Lamb" and not want to raise my hands to him.

> *Lord, make us grateful for the sacrifice of your Son, Jesus Christ. Help us to remember that he is the willing, sacrificial, triumphant Lamb who died for us. The King of Kings and Lord of Lords took the bullet so that we could live forever with you. Thank you.*

Application

1. "The key doctrine of Christianity is that Jesus died on the cross. He was the atoning sacrifice for everything you have ever done wrong, are doing wrong right now, and any wrong you will ever commit." What sins has Christ covered for you?
2. "We often compare ourselves with one another. It's hard not to. We compare our goodness to other people's goodness. Sometimes we go away feeling pretty good about ourselves." To whom do you compare your "goodness"? How does that minimize the greatness of Jesus' work in your life?
3. "Jesus died for all those people in India. They, along with others all around the world, need to hear that he is the Lamb, their ultimate sacrifice." With whom has God called you to share the news of Jesus' life-giving sacrifice? Have you done it?
4. "That is the triumphant Christ, who changes the heart and changes the face, the Lamb of God who takes away the sin of the world." How has the Lamb of God changed your heart and life? How does he continue to change your heart and life?
5. "We all deserved death for our sins. Jesus paid our penalty, yet I wonder how grateful we really are

that he did." When did you last thank God for the
sacrifice of his Son? How do you show him your
appreciation and gratefulness?

Jesus, Our Savior

Chapter 4

THE TEACHER

THERE WAS A MAN OF THE PHARISEE SECT, NICODEMUS, A PROMINENT LEADER AMONG THE JEWS. LATE ONE NIGHT HE VISITED JESUS AND SAID, "RABBI, WE ALL KNOW YOU'RE A TEACHER STRAIGHT FROM GOD. NO ONE COULD DO ALL THE GOD-POINTING, GOD-REVEALING ACTS YOU DO IF GOD WEREN'T IN ON IT."

JESUS SAID, "YOU'RE ABSOLUTELY RIGHT. TAKE IT FROM ME: UNLESS A PERSON IS BORN FROM ABOVE, IT'S NOT POSSIBLE TO SEE WHAT I'M POINTING TO—TO GOD'S KINGDOM."

—JOHN 3:1–3 MSG

Many have called Jesus the greatest teacher ever to live. He is our example of how to teach. He could hold the attention of his listeners, no matter their age. The parables he taught have been told and retold for generations.

In John 3, Nicodemus approaches Jesus, the great teacher. Sometimes we gloss over this story, but a closer look reveals why this was such an amazing encounter. We see in this story the qualities that made Jesus such a wonderful teacher.

Jesus Was Approachable

Nicodemus was from the upper class, a leader, and a member of the ruling council. He was so prominent that, in verse 10, Jesus refers to him as "Israel's teacher." As a Pharisee, however, he led a legalistic lifestyle, holding on to the Old Testament law and man-made traditions that had developed among the Jews over the years. Nicodemus was the one with all the answers to people's questions.

We all know people like Nicodemus, people who believe their way of thinking is the only way to think. There are even ministers like that. In several of his books, Philip Yancey exposes the damage that dogmatic, legalistic pastors have done. They wield Scripture as a tool of manipulation, and they use guilt as a weapon.

Nicodemus might have been very closed minded when it came to new ideas, but something about Jesus gnawed at him. So he came to see Jesus at night. Many theologians have supposed that Nicodemus was afraid of what his peers might think of him going to see Jesus, prompting him to wait for the cover of night. It could also be, however, that he was smart and knew that people surrounded Jesus during the day. Perhaps that's why he sought him in the evening, when he could easily have a private audience with him.

An even more thought-provoking possibility is that he came at night because he was a teacher of the law, and many teachers at that time did a great deal of their studying at night. Today we still have college students who stay up well into the night to churn out a paper or study for a test!

The main point, however, is that Nicodemus went to see

Jesus. He must have heard much about this new teacher. He believed Jesus would receive him and listen to him.

Charles Templeton, who traveled extensively with Billy Graham back in the 1950s, eventually drifted away from the faith. He even wrote a book called *Farewell to God: My Reasons for Rejecting the Christian Faith*. Shortly before his death, he granted an interview to Lee Strobel, in which he explained his reasons for walking away from the Lord.

In his book *The Case for Faith*, Strobel quotes Templeton:

> [I saw] a picture of a black woman in Northern Africa.... They were experiencing a devastating drought. And she was holding her dead baby in her arms and looking up to heaven with the most forlorn expression. I looked at it and I thought, "Is it possible to believe that there is a loving or caring Creator when all this woman needed was rain?"
>
> Then I began to think further about the world being the creation of God. I started considering the plagues that sweep across parts of the planet and indiscriminately kill—more often than not, painfully—all kinds of people, the ordinary, the decent, and the rotten. And it just became crystal clear to me that it is not possible for an intelligent person to believe that there is a deity who loves.[1]

Charles Templeton could not reconcile this problem in his mind. He could not understand why God would let bad things happen to good people. It kept him from approaching Jesus, in whom he had previously believed.

What keeps us from approaching Christ? Doubts? Time? Pride? Self-love? Shame? We don't have to come by night. We can come before God at any time to pour out our hearts. Hebrews 4:16 says, "Let us then approach the throne of grace with confidence, so that we may receive mercy and find grace to help us in our time of need."

Jesus Was Unique

We like teachers who are different, who think differently, and teach in a manner that goes beyond the ordinary and mundane. Our son Ben wanted to take guitar lessons, so we set up a meeting with a prospective teacher. From the moment we got there, I knew something was up. The room was bare, with nothing on the walls, and nothing inside but two chairs, two amps, and Rod. With his long beard and worn-out shorts and tennis shoes, Rod looked like he could have come straight off the downtown streets.

When we asked what kind of guitar he was holding, Rod explained that he had made it. I was starting to get uneasy! In my less-than-subtle way, I asked about his credentials. He had a master's degree in music with an emphasis in guitar performance from Oregon State University. *Well, he can't be that bad*, I thought.

Rod turned to Ben. "So who do you want to play like?" he asked.

"Eric Clapton and Carlos Santana," Ben immediately replied. Rod smiled, picked up his guitar, and for the next five minutes played stuff that confirmed to us that he was going to be Ben's guitar teacher. He was unique and extremely talented. I'm glad we didn't just turn and leave after our first look at him.

The uniqueness of Jesus drew Nicodemus to him. He recognized that Jesus was something special. He said, "Rabbi, we know you are a teacher who has come from God. For no one could perform the miraculous signs you are doing if God were not with him" (John 3:2).

Notice how Nicodemus addressed Jesus: *Rabbi*. The root of the word means "great" or "my great one." It was a title of dignity and respect for those who taught and gave counsel. During the time of Jesus, the Jews used it to address their spiritual teachers. The Pharisees, of course, reveled in it. In our modern world, *rabbi* still refers to one who has been trained for professional religious leadership and possesses authority to interpret God's law.

The title caused some problems in Jesus' time. The rabbis used their authority to dominate and control others, particularly in their faith.

Jesus rebuked the Pharisees' abuse of power, saying, "They tie up heavy loads and put them on men's shoulders, but they themselves are not willing to lift a finger to move them.... They love to be greeted in the marketplaces and to have men call them 'Rabbi.' But you are not to be called 'Rabbi,' for you have only one Master and you are all brothers" (Matt. 23:4, 7–8).

Nicodemus used the term *rabbi* with great respect. He believed that Jesus was truly a good teacher. Why? Because of the miraculous signs he had been doing. Maybe Nicodemus had seen the healing touch of Jesus. Or perhaps he had heard testimony from someone he knew and trusted. Nicodemus knew Jesus could do such amazing miracles only by the power of God. No other rabbi could do what Jesus did. He was unique.

Jesus Was Perceptive

Good teachers know whether or not their students are "getting it." But when a teacher asks, "Do you get it?" a student may seek to avoid embarrassment with an insincere "yes." So, a good teacher will look more closely at the students to determine if they *really* get it.

Jesus knew his visitor didn't "get it." Nicodemus doesn't even get the chance to ask a question before Jesus says, "I tell you the truth, no one can see the kingdom of God unless he is born again" (John 3:3). Jesus discerned Nicodemus's deeper question and the doubts that had long haunted him, even though he was "Israel's teacher." People saw him as the authority on life after death. But Nicodemus himself was uncertain he had it right.

Maybe it was because he was getting older or just that he had begun to think seriously about his own mortality. Whatever the reason, Nicodemus had an important question on his mind, which Jesus succinctly addressed.

Most people don't like to think about life's end and want to avoid that conversation like the plague itself. But most of us, as we grow older, inevitably start to wonder about what is "on the other side."

Jesus had the answer for Nicodemus. "I tell you the truth, no one can see the kingdom of God unless he is born again." He basically said, "Listen, I know what is on your mind and your heart. I know you are a true seeker. I know you want to see God and be with God at the end of your journey. So here it is: You must be born again. Yes, you were birthed into this world physically; now you need to be birthed spiritually. My Father's kingdom is a spiritual kingdom and entry to it requires a new heart, a new allegiance, a new birth."

As Leon Morris writes in his commentary on John, "In one sentence he [Jesus] sweeps away all that Nicodemus stood for and demands that he be re-made by the power of God."[2] Nicodemus had to understand that entry into the kingdom of God does not come by works or human effort, but by a rebirth that only God can affect. That is the message Jesus came to bring.

How do you view that message? Has it lost its meaning and power in your life? Or do you thank God every day for sending his Son to die so that simply by believing we receive a spot in heaven forever?

Jesus Was Caring

Did you ever receive a syllabus—a summary of a course of study—when you were in college? There are a lot of teachers who love to use a syllabus. It gives them a road map for the whole semester. Unfortunately, this often causes the students to do only the bare minimum; after all, the syllabus tells them exactly what they need to do to get a passing grade. I always got more out of the teachers who would leave me hanging a little bit instead of just dumping their syllabus on me.

Jesus' way of teaching is very interesting. He does not put it all out there in one statement or one discourse. He doesn't provide all the answers in one lecture. He allows just enough mystery to keep the person coming back for more.

Nicodemus asks Jesus a question that is full of emotion. He is having a hard time grasping what Jesus has said. Jesus does not blow him off or belittle him—he doesn't even seem perturbed by this question. He cares for Nicodemus, and he knows his heart. He realizes Nicodemus is truly seeking. He is on a spiritual quest.

Is it okay to question Jesus? Is it okay to question God? When bad things happen to us, when innocent people are brutally murdered, when families lose everything to fire or flood, and when hardworking fathers lose their jobs, we often ask, "Why, God?"

There are, however, four conditions that must be met before we question God. First, we must have hearts that truly want to understand God better. Second, we must understand that God does not have to operate according to our human standards. Third, we must accept the fact that we may not like his answers. Fourth, we must accept that he may answer with silence.

Jesus Clarified What He Meant

What subjects were hard for you in school? I had a hard time with math. The only class I ever flunked was algebra. The only reason I need math is to manage my money, so I won't have to choose which of my sons to live with thirty years from now. But I also had struggles at various times with other subjects. I truly did hate school.

There is nothing worse than sitting in class while the teacher tries to teach a concept you just don't get. You ask a question and receive an answer, but you still don't get it. Yet it seems like everyone else does. Then when you get your test back, you really see how much you didn't get it. So after school you go to see the teacher for extra help.

Mrs. Eberling was my eighth-grade biology teacher. She was fun. We got to see lots of movies in her class. But one day she saw my test and realized I didn't *get it*. So after class, she took me aside and slowly went over it, breaking it down until I *got* the whole photosynthesis concept. What a thrill to have the lights go on! She was happy and so was I.

With Nicodemus, the light still hadn't come on, so Jesus drew him in a little bit further. He explains that a believer must be born of water and spirit. Birth by water refers to the physical birth process. We enter the *world* by physical birth, but we enter God's *kingdom* by spiritual birth. The Holy Spirit, who gives birth to us, then illuminates our minds so we can understand the things of God. We ought to stop and thank God for allowing us to understand our need for him. Faith is a gift. Jesus is God's way of showing himself to us so that we "get it."

Jesus Was Convincing

To explain further what he meant, Jesus uses an illustration Nicodemus can better understand. Perhaps a breeze began to blow as they were talking. So he compares the work of God to the wind. Then Jesus speaks about a new kind of spiritual experience that Nicodemus needed. This thought should not have been foreign to Nicodemus. The Lord says in Ezekiel 36:25–27, "I will sprinkle clean water on you, and you will be clean; I will cleanse you from all your impurities and from all your idols. I will give you a new heart and put a new spirit in you; I will remove from you your heart of stone and give you a heart of flesh. And I will put my Spirit in you and move you to follow my decrees and be careful to keep my laws."

Jesus' words have an impact on Nicodemus. He begins to understand that conformity and legalism are not enough to get him into the kingdom. He starts to understand that God is not impressed with his self-discipline, that even his best efforts are not God honoring, but rooted in selfish pride.

To what degree do we perform simply because we think it impresses God? One spring day I was sitting in my home when I saw someone come to the door. She didn't ring the doorbell, so I went to the door later to see what she had left. It was an invitation to go to church on Easter. I thought of the times I've done that, but not with the thought that someone might come to Christ. I wondered instead how much God would appreciate that I sacrificed an afternoon to go pass out invitations to church.

At various times we are all like Nicodemus. We sometimes do things for God, not out of selfless devotion, but because we think it will earn us favor with him. Many times in the Gospels, after an encounter with Christ, people have to make a choice. The rich young ruler chose to walk away. The nine lepers did not return to give glory to God. Those who followed Jesus for food quickly went the other way. Their hearts never changed; there was not a new Spirit within them.

Do you see a change in yourself? Has a relationship with Christ made a difference not just in your life but in your heart?

We don't see much of Nicodemus in the rest of the Gospels, but we do know that at some point the light came on. We find him weakly defending Jesus in John 7:50–53. He then helps Joseph of Arimathea bury Jesus in John 19:39. Slowly, over time, Nicodemus comes to understand the message Jesus had told him that night. Some people cannot identify a specific time when they came to Christ. That's okay. The important thing is that the Holy Spirit convicts them over a period of time and that they eventually believe.

J. B. Phillips writes, "Every time we say, 'I believe in the Holy Spirit,' we mean that we believe that there is a living God able and willing to enter human personality and change it."[3] F. F. Bruce writes in his commentary on the gospel of John, "The hidden work of the Spirit in the human heart cannot be controlled or seen, but its effects are unmistakably evident."[4]

My wife, Deb, teaches our youngest son at home. Although she loves to watch him learn as he does his schoolwork, her greatest joy is seeing him take what he has learned and make good life decisions. Jesus must get excited when our Monday behavior matches our Sunday spirituality. After all, anybody can put on an act for a couple of hours on Sunday morning. But the real question is, are we making progress during the week? Jesus, the great teacher, never stops teaching. What does he want to teach you today? Do you need to learn humility or kindness or patience? Do you need to work on loving others more?

The thing that brings the most joy to a teacher is seeing his students succeed. Jesus wants us to succeed in our Christian lives. To do that, however, we need to come to him and ask questions—like Nicodemus did—about what we don't understand. We can then trust him to guide us.

Jesus, you are the greatest teacher who ever lived. Help us to be diligent students of your Word, never ceasing to search for the truth. Thank you for being our guide to the truth.

Application

1. "Nicodemus might have been very closed minded when it came to new ideas." In what areas of your life are you legalistic or closed minded? How does Jesus call you to think differently in those areas?
2. "Nicodemus went to see Jesus. He must have heard much about this new teacher." What have you heard or learned about Jesus that compels you to seek him?

3. "Nicodemus asks Jesus a question that is full of emotion. He is having a hard time grasping what Jesus has said." What has Jesus said to you that has been difficult for you to understand or act upon? How has he helped you understand?

4. "We are all like Nicodemus. We sometimes do things for God, not out of selfless devotion, but because we think it will earn us favor with him." What is your motivation for doing things for God? Do you need to reevaluate your acts of service?

5. "F. F. Bruce writes in his commentary on the gospel of John, 'The hidden work of the Spirit in the human heart cannot be controlled or seen, but its effects are unmistakably evident.'" What evidence of the Spirit's work in your heart do you see in your life?

CHAPTER 5

THE SON OF GOD

THIS IS HOW MUCH GOD LOVED THE WORLD: HE GAVE HIS SON, HIS ONE AND ONLY SON. AND THIS IS WHY: SO THAT NO ONE NEED BE DESTROYED; BY BELIEVING IN HIM, ANYONE CAN HAVE A WHOLE AND LASTING LIFE. GOD DIDN'T GO TO ALL THE TROUBLE OF SENDING HIS SON MERELY TO POINT AN ACCUSING FINGER, TELLING THE WORLD HOW BAD IT WAS. HE CAME TO HELP, TO PUT THE WORLD RIGHT AGAIN. ANYONE WHO TRUSTS IN HIM IS ACQUITTED; ANYONE WHO REFUSES TO TRUST HIM HAS LONG SINCE BEEN UNDER THE DEATH SENTENCE WITHOUT KNOWING IT. AND WHY? BECAUSE OF THAT PERSON'S FAILURE TO BELIEVE IN THE ONE-OF-A-KIND SON OF GOD WHEN INTRODUCED TO HIM.

—JOHN 3:16–18 MSG

John 3:16 may be the most famous verse in the Bible. Hundreds of millions of people around the globe have cherished this verse for nearly two thousand years because it tells us about God's great love for us. After his encounter with Nicodemus, Jesus begins to reveal the amazing plan that God has to redeem the world. He sent his very own Son!

Do *you* know that God loves you? I mean, do you *really* know that God loves you with a deep, passionate, sacrificial, pure, and unshakable love? He loved us so much that he sent his only Son, the Son he loved, to die for our sins.

Look within the verse, and what do we know?

- We know there is a **God.**
- We know that this God doesn't hate **the world.**
- We know that this God **loves** the world.
- We know that this God, who loves the world, must be a Father because he has a **Son.**
- We know that this God must **love** the world a great deal because he **gave** one of the greatest gifts he could possibly give—his **one and only Son.**
- We know that **whoever believes** in this Son will not suffer the terrible consequence of **perishing.**
- We know that whoever believes in this Son will receive the wonderful gift of having **eternal life.**

These basic truths, however, don't tell us everything we need to know. If it's so important to believe in God's one and only Son, who is he?

The relationship between Jesus the Son and God the Father is unique and communicates some important truths. Have you ever wondered about the significance of Jesus' identity as God's Son? Why did God send Jesus to the world as his *Son*?

A Son Demonstrates the Father's Love

When Jesus said, "God so loved the world," the Jews must have been stunned. They knew that God loved *them*. The Jewish people had a history with God. They were counting on the fact that God loved them. But the rest of the world? Every nation, every culture, every subculture—even the foreigner, the half-breed, the imperfect, the poor—the whole world? How could God love all of them, too?

That statement must have been hard for them to grasp. It must have especially irritated the Pharisees, who thought that God loved *them* the most. Remember the Pharisee's prayer? "God, I thank you that I am not like other men—robbers, evil-doers, adulterers—or even like this tax collector. I fast twice a week and give a tenth of all I get" (Luke 18:11–12). The Pharisees prided themselves on their outstanding reputation before God.

Jesus declares that God's love is broad enough to encompass the whole world—even the sinners of the world. There is no spiritual elite in this new covenant. Commentator F. F. Bruce writes,

> If there is one sentence more than another which sums up the message of the Fourth Gospel, it is this. The love of God is limitless; it embraces all mankind ... the best that God had to give, he gave—his only Son, his well-beloved ... he was given so that all, without distinction or exception ... might be rescued from destruction and blessed with the life that is life indeed.[1]

The abundant love of God should never cease to amaze us!

The thought of how much God loves us, in light of our sinfulness, ought to humble us. How could he keep on loving humans, who so often rebel and desert him? C. S. Lewis puts it well: "God, who needs nothing, loves into existence wholly superfluous creatures in order that he may love and perfect them."[2]

Several years ago, I came across Henri Nouwen's classic book *The Return of the Prodigal Son*. While I realize that he was a

Catholic priest and we would probably not agree on every point of theology, his book had a profound impact on me. Nouwen uses the familiar story of the prodigal son from Luke 15 as well as Rembrandt's painting of the prodigal's return to bring God's love into full view. Nouwen wrote:

> As I let all of it sink in, I see how the story of the father and his lost son powerfully affirms that it was not I who chose God, but God who first chose me. This is the great mystery of our faith. We do not choose God, God chooses us. From all eternity we are hidden "in the shadow of God's hand" and "engraved on his palm." Before any human being touches us, God "forms us in secret" and "textures us" in the depth of the earth, and before any human being decides about us, God "knits us together in our mother's womb." God loves us before any human person can show love to us. He loves us with a "first" love, an unlimited love, wants us to be his beloved children, and tells us to become as loving as himself.[3]

Once, at the beginning of our Sunday service, our pastor asked us to turn to the other members of the congregation and say, "God is fond of you." It was a little uncomfortable for some people. Would you find it difficult to say that? How sad it is that so many people in this world think that they are too poor, too sinful, too broken, too lost for God to care about them. But God never says that! Peter writes that the Lord is "not wanting anyone to perish, but everyone to come to repentance" (2 Peter 3:9).

God loved the world—the whole world—so much that he sent his Son to die for us. He is actively seeking a relationship with us. Are we allowing him to find us? It requires honesty, vulnerability, and a heart that is open to him.

Perhaps it's easier for a parent to understand the depth of the Father's love for his Son and for all of us, his children.

When my wife and I had our first child, back in the day before the doctors could tell you what sex the baby is, Deb really wanted a girl. She had never had brothers and didn't know what she would do with a boy. I wanted a boy, because I was a youth pastor at the time and I had trouble dealing with all the teenage girls; they always seemed to have so many problems.

When our baby entered the world and the doctor announced that it was a boy, Deb confessed she was a little disappointed, but not for long. She formed an instant bond with our son and loved him immensely. What an amazing experience it was for us!

If the love of God is a mystery, then the fact that he sent Jesus to embody that love is an even greater one. In Philippians 2, we find God's plan in capsule form. Many scholars believe Paul was actually quoting a hymn that believers sang in the early church. It offers great insight into what the early church believed about Jesus:

> Your attitude should be the same as that of Christ
> Jesus:
> Who, being in very nature God,
>   did not consider equality with God something
>   to be grasped,
> but made himself nothing,
>   taking the very nature of a servant,
>   being made in human likeness.
> And being found in appearance as a man,
>   he humbled himself
>   and became obedient to death—
>   even death on a cross!
> Therefore God exalted him to the highest place
>   and gave him the name that is above every
>   name,
> that at the name of Jesus every knee should bow,
>   in heaven and on earth and under the earth,
> and every tongue confess that Jesus Christ is Lord,
>   to the glory of God the Father. (vv. 5–11)

Someone has said, "Jesus did not come to make God's love possible, but to make God's love visible." Romans 5:8 explains, "God demonstrates his own love for us in this: While we were still sinners, Christ died for us."

Jesus shows how great the Father's love is. God didn't send Jesus to die for us because we were wonderful people or because we had something to offer him. He loved us so much that he gave up his Son for that love alone! How amazing!

The Son Is the Same in Essence

Two of my sons are now young adults. They are individuals with their own gifts, passions, and personalities. Even though they no longer live in the same home with me, and even though they make their own plans, they can never get very far from me. They are a part of me. They have my DNA in them. They reflect my personality, my strengths, and my weaknesses.

In an even more profound way, Jesus Christ is the essence of the Father. He is God revealed in human form. He was "in very nature God."

Humanly speaking, Jesus' claim to be the Son of God is what got him crucified. The Jews considered it blasphemy for any man to claim equality with God, which is what Christ was doing when he called himself God's Son. He had the same essence. Even though the Old Testament had repeatedly predicted that God would send a Savior, the Jews were not expecting someone like Jesus to come along—a poor, simple carpenter claiming to be the "I AM" just like the Father.

Jesus never claimed to be pious, a divine, a moralist, or simply a great teacher. He claimed to be God in the flesh, with a divine mission to atone for the sins of the world. That boggled and enraged the minds of the Jews:

Again the Jews picked up stones to stone him, but Jesus said to them, "I have shown you many great miracles from the Father. For which of these do you stone me?"

"We are not stoning you for any of these," replied the Jews, "but for blasphemy, because you, a mere man, claim to be God." (John 10:31–33)

I once read a book entitled *American Jesus: How the Son of God Became a National Icon* by Stephen Prothero, chairman of the Department of Religion at Boston University. In a review of that book, Tim Berroth said, "As a scholar and historian, Prothero's painstaking research paints an often hilarious, sometimes painfully convicting picture of how our nation has sliced, diced, molded, and re-shaped God the Son into everything but the Savior of sinful man."[4]

A Son Is Obedient

Children are supposed to obey their parents. That is the way God has decreed we should live. Seeing disobedient little children who mouth off to their parents is an ugly sight. Watching parents try to reason with a screaming, rebellious child is sad. If only parents would listen to what God has said about how to raise children, life would be so much easier for them.

The country of Singapore has a low crime rate, partly due to the fact that their society clearly defines and consistently enforces its rules. Children are not allowed to get away with whatever they want.

I read an article about an eighteen-year-old American named Michael Fay who, in 1994, went on a vandalism spree in Singapore. He vandalized two cars with eggs and spray paint. The authorities caught him and found him guilty of more than fifty acts of vandalism. His punishment was six whacks on the buttocks with a rattan cane, four months in jail, and a fine of around $3,000.

America went crazy. Our ambassador tried to appeal, dozens of congressman tried to appeal, and even President Clinton tried to save Michael, but to no avail. The media in our country portrayed Singapore as a horrible place. Of course, anyone who has spent time there would have just shrugged his shoulders and said, "He knew the rules and he defied them. He is getting what he deserves."

Newsweek magazine later published a response from S. B. Balachandrer, press secretary to the Ministry for Home Affairs in Singapore. He wrote,

> Your report, "Six Lashes in Singapore" (U.S. Affairs, March 14) gives the impression that Michael Fay's crimes consisted merely of "disfiguring two cars with eggs and spray paint." The list of offenses committed by Fay, an American, runs much longer. He had initially been charged with a total of 53 counts of vandalism and related offenses. However, after plea bargaining, he was charged with two counts of vandalism, two counts of mischief and one count of stolen property—all of which he pleaded guilty to. In passing sentence on Fay, the court also took into consideration his admission to 16 other counts of vandalism and four counts of mischief. Twenty-seven counts of vandalism and one count of possession of dangerous fireworks were withdrawn as a result of the plea bargaining. In the last five years, 12 Singaporeans and two foreigners have been sentenced to caning for vandalism. In upholding the law, Singapore treats both Singaporeans and foreigners alike.[5]

That young man knew what was at stake. He broke the rules anyway, and he paid the price.

Jesus Christ knew the rules, and he knew what was at stake. He obeyed his Father. The press could have said it was unfair that Jesus was going to be put on a cross; local human rights groups and moralists could have stepped up the pressure to prevent such a horrible death. But God the Father and God the Son knew from the beginning what his mission on earth was all about. Jesus was the obedient Son who wanted what his Father wanted.

"For God so loved the world that he gave his one and only Son, that whoever believes in him shall not perish but have eternal life." If you don't have that verse memorized, I encourage you to read it over and over again until you do.

This is how much God loved us: He sent his Son, his only Son. Have you thanked him for that incredible gift today?

Father, thank you for showing your love to the whole world through the gift of your Son. Jesus, thank you for willingly obeying the Father, even at the cost of your life. Help us to always stand in thankful amazement of your sacrifice.

Application

1. "Jesus declares that God's love is broad enough to encompass the whole world—even the sinners of the world. There is no spiritual elite in this new covenant." How does the knowledge that God does not play favorites humble you? Do you treat others as equally worthy of God's love?
2. "[God] is actively seeking a relationship with us.... It requires honesty, vulnerability, and a heart that is open to him." What kind of relationship do you have with the Father? Are you honest, vulnerable, and real before him?
3. "Children are supposed to obey their parents. That is the way God has decreed we should live." As God's child, do you obey his commands? In what ways do you struggle with obedience to him?
4. "Jesus was the obedient Son who wanted what his Father wanted." Do your desires conform to God's desires? Do you want what he wants?

CHAPTER 6

THE BREAD OF LIFE

JESUS SAID, "I AM THE BREAD OF LIFE. THE PERSON WHO ALIGNS WITH ME HUNGERS NO MORE AND THIRSTS NO MORE, EVER. I HAVE TOLD YOU THIS EXPLICITLY BECAUSE EVEN THOUGH YOU HAVE SEEN ME IN ACTION, YOU DON'T REALLY BELIEVE ME. EVERY PERSON THE FATHER GIVES ME EVENTUALLY COMES RUNNING TO ME. AND ONCE THAT PERSON IS WITH ME, I HOLD ON AND DON'T LET GO. I CAME DOWN FROM HEAVEN NOT TO FOLLOW MY OWN WHIM BUT TO ACCOMPLISH THE WILL OF THE ONE WHO SENT ME."

—JOHN 6:35–38 MSG

Bread is an important part of life. It is a simple, yet nourishing, substance that has sustained people for thousands of years.

Sadly, there are millions of people in the world who go hungry every day. At least five million children under the age of five will die this year from malnutrition. Out of the 6.2 billion people on this earth, 1.2 billion live on less than $1 a day.[1]

Still, when we talk about famine and hunger in our world, many of us don't even give it a second thought—even when there are plenty of children right here in America who go to bed hungry every night.

In 2002, Bono, lead singer of the rock band U2, spoke at a banquet for Africare, a nonprofit organization specializing in bringing aid to Africa. Bono called the attitude of the West toward famine and hunger a "supertanker of indifference." He said, "We can't choose the benefits of globalization without some of the responsibilities, and we should remind ourselves that 'love thy neighbor' is not advice: it is a command."[2] We in the West have so much money and resources. So why aren't we doing more to eradicate hunger in the world?

In our country, where we have more of a problem with obesity than nearly any other country, food is easy to obtain. We go to a grocery store and pick up whatever we need. I still remember the first time a friend from India visited me. I took him to a Safeway supermarket; he was in absolute awe of how much food is available to us at any time. Not just one cookie, but thirty different varieties of cookies!

We're not accustomed to dealing with hunger. Most of us don't concern ourselves with such tasks as planting and harvesting produce, raising and slaughtering cattle. Why go to that much work when we can head over to our local grocery store and pull what we need off a shelf? When we want bread, we choose from several different kinds. For many other people all over the world, simply to have a piece of bread means they will live another day.

Jesus says, "I am the bread of life." John 6:35 is the first time he uses the words "I am." He uses those same words again in verse 41: "I am the bread that came down from heaven." Then again in verses 48 and 51: "I am the bread of life," and "I am the living bread that came down from heaven."

The crowd Jesus addresses is the same crowd of five thousand he earlier had fed with bread and fish. They have followed him to the opposite side of the lake and ask, "Rabbi, when did you get here?" (6:25). Jesus replies, "I tell you the truth, you are looking for me, not because you saw miraculous signs but because you ate the loaves and had your fill" (v. 26). Jesus then instructs them, "Do not work for food that spoils, but for food that endures to eternal life, which the Son of Man will give you. On him God the Father has placed his seal of approval" (v. 27).

The work that God requires is very simple. Jesus explains that it is "to believe in the one he has sent" (v. 29). But the crowd wants another sign in order to believe. They mistakenly say that Moses gave them bread from heaven in the wilderness. But Jesus says it is God who gives bread from heaven. They ask Jesus to give them this bread, and again Jesus declares, "I am the bread of life. He who comes to me will never go hungry, and he who believes in me will never be thirsty" (v. 35).

Jesus had fed the multitudes. He had multiplied fish and loaves. These people were witnesses of that great sign. Jesus left that place the next day and walked across the lake. The crowd tracked him down. Why? The day before they had their bellies filled. They had seen a miracle. Now they're hungry again and wanted Jesus to repeat the favor.

Jesus immediately realizes why they have come. He is saying, "You're not coming after me because you want me. You're not coming after me because you want God. You're coming after me because you want some material blessing; that's why you're seeking me."

Jesus uses this opportunity to teach them a spiritual lesson. He wants to give them insight into their true condition, to teach them that *he* is the bread from heaven, the Bread of Life. The people were overcome by their materialism. They were overcome by the thinking that they could, by their deeds, please God. Their thinking was, "Just tell us what works we need to do, and we'll do them." Jesus says, "No, it's not about works. It's about believing." They were proud, thinking they could do whatever it took to get to God. But Jesus is saying, "No, it starts and ends with me."

What does the Bread of Life mean to us today? Every one of us needs the Bread of Life. There is a hunger inside of us, and we need this bread. Consider what Jesus came to offer us.

The Bread of Life Saves Us

The crowd came to Jesus, wanting to manipulate him by asking for a sign. Of course, he had already given them a sign. Hadn't he already fed the five thousand? Yet they say to him, "Okay, give us *another* sign. Maybe then we'll follow you." What they were really saying was, "Hey, we admit what you did the other day was really cool, but our forefathers followed Moses, and Moses brought down manna for forty consecutive years. It shouldn't be too hard for you to do it again, right?"

Jesus says, "I'm not going to have any part of this." He ignores their request and makes two important clarifications. First, he points out that the manna, the food from heaven that Moses gave the children of Israel, did not come from Moses. It came from God.

Second, he points out that the manna was not the true bread. The word *true* means "genuine" or "original." *Jesus* is the real bread. He wants the people to realize that *he* is the Bread of Life and that, if they believe in him, they will never spiritually hunger again.

In my travels around the world, I've seen a lot of hungry people. When people are literally starving to death, there is a desperation that goes beyond anything that we really know about. They would do anything to have one little morsel to eat, one slice of bread to save them for another day. Most of us have never known that kind of desperation. The people who came to Jesus that day were not desperate. They were self-sufficient.

"Oh, we can do the works of God. Yeah, we can do whatever you want us to do. And, by the way, we need you to show us your credentials one more time."

Some people have never been desperate for God. They don't know what it's like really to hunger for him. There are others who have been extremely desperate for God, hungering for him day after day. They cry out, "God, show yourself to me," and following God is their greatest passion.

John Piper wrote, "The key to Christian living is a thirst and hunger for God."[3] Many people do not understand or experience God's sovereign grace and the way it awakens sovereign joy because their hunger and thirst for God are so small.

We are too easily satisfied with our Christianity. We're happy to go to church, sing a few songs, listen to a nice message, and then go home and get back to our normal lives. A passion, desperation, and intense hunger for God are just not a part of our experience.

Many of us enjoy church. We like the music, the friends we meet, and having a place to belong. When we leave after Sunday services, it makes us feel good that we've "been to church." Oh yes. We've experienced church. But when was the last time we truly encountered God, with Jesus, the Bread of Life? If I've never had that encounter with Jesus, it doesn't matter how often I go to church. It doesn't matter what Bible study I attend or in what ministry I serve. I'll still be dissatisfied. I'll still be hungry in my soul until God himself satisfies that hunger.

When I started Eternity Minded Ministries several years ago, we sent out letters that invited people to support the ministry. There was one middle-aged couple who decided they were going to contribute. I knew Joe and Melinda from a church in San Diego. He had started his own business, which was doing well. They wrote me a note that said, "Dan, we're going to support you $100 a month from here on out." I thought, *Wow, that's a lot of money. Praise the Lord!*

Not only were they generous, but Joe and Melinda were also very involved in their church. She was a secretary, and he had served as a deacon for many years. For a while he was an elder, providing spiritual leadership to the church. They were strongly connected with that church family.

I heard some time after they made that support commitment that Joe had decided to give his heart to Jesus Christ. When I heard that, I smiled and thought about what courage, what humility, what hunger and desperation it took for a man who was a leader in the church to bow before the Lord and admit, "I don't really know you. It's now time to know you."

Jesus, the bread, saves us. He told those Jews, "Listen, the bread, the manna from heaven that you ate—it was good, but those people still died eventually even though they ate it. But the bread that I'm going to give you is the bread that will give you eternal life."

Now that I'm older, I have had to face death more frequently. Family and friends have passed away—and it is such a hard time, a grieving time. But as I told my wife, Deb, the other day, it's good for my spiritual journey. Why? Because when someone you know dies, it makes you think about the reality of heaven and about the reality of knowing God. You think about it more than you normally would. You can't get your mind off God because you're thinking so much about your loved one being in the presence of God. And we think about how wonderful it will be to see our loved one in heaven with God.

Jesus said, "I am the bread, and I am the one that gives eternal life." The Bread of Life saves us.

The Bread of Life Satisfies Us

The crowd got hungry, and they came looking for more food. Jesus' miracle had been a temporary fix.

Life is full of temporary fixes. I have learned that when I get stressed out I do two things: I eat more and I spend more. Those are not good. Those coping mechanisms will get you into trouble really fast. When I eat more or spend more, I feel better but only for a brief moment of time. Then I feel worse.

Jesus promises to satisfy us in those stressful and difficult times. The Bread of Life meets our every need. Television advertisements promise fulfillment but fail to deliver. They play off our heartache, loneliness, depression, and emptiness. They say, "If you buy this, you will feel better." We have all believed them at times. I have done that, and I didn't feel any better in the long run. In the end we discover that it's all just slick marketing.

Jesus says, "Come to me, all you who are weary and burdened, and I will give you rest" (Matt. 11:28). He will give rest to you—the real you, where the real heartache is, where the real desperation is, and where the real loneliness is. Material things won't give you rest. They won't fill your need. They can't make you happy in the long run. Jesus says, "*I* am the Bread of Life and *I* satisfy."

I read in the newspaper about a successful dentist who ran down her husband with her Mercedes-Benz when she found out he was having an affair. She is now serving a twenty-year prison sentence. She has twin four-year-olds. The article reported all the ways she tried to keep her husband and their relationship. But he kept playing around behind her back, and she finally snapped. As I read that, I thought, *Lord, they both needed the Bread of Life. They needed you because both of them were so dissatisfied with life*. But they never discovered that Jesus is the bread that satisfies.

I've sometimes wondered about the satisfaction Jesus offers. "Okay, he brings *eternal* life, but does he have any impact on my life right now?" Maybe you've found yourself asking a similar question. "Does Jesus have any reality in my life today? Can Jesus really satisfy my soul at this very moment?" The answer is yes.

Jesus said in Matthew 5:6, "Blessed are those who hunger and thirst for righteousness, for they shall be satisfied" (NASB).

When we hunger and thirst for him, he will satisfy our hearts. No position, no recognition, no financial security will be able to do that. Only Jesus can do that for you. Isaiah 55:2 admonishes, "Why spend money on what is not bread, and your labor on what does not satisfy?" That is the issue. I love it when somebody is honest enough to say, "Hey, I'm a follower of Jesus, but I'm just not satisfied." That person's honesty is the first step toward finding satisfaction. As long as we keep being self-sufficient, and as long as we keep being the one who has all the answers, we'll never know what that satisfaction is.

We may allow God to save us, but we often do not allow him to satisfy us. We cry out, "God, save me, but that's about as far as I want to go." The psalmist had more than that in mind when he wrote, "As the deer pants for streams of water, so my soul pants for you, O God. My soul thirsts for God, for the living God. When can I go and meet with God?" (42:1–2).

When you wake up on Sunday morning and you think about going to church, enjoying the music and the worship, I pray that you think, *I'm going to meet with God.* That's what should be in our minds when we go to church. I confess it's not always in my mind. There are times I regard it as my duty.

Whenever you go to church, whether it's Saturday or Sunday or Wednesday or any other day, say to God, "I'm here to meet with you. I'm hungry for you to speak to me and minister to me." Our hunger for God is one of the greatest evidences that we have to know we are one of his. If there is no hunger, there should be a red flag in our minds because that hunger for him, that desire to know him, is very important to our relationship with God. Some people just want heaven. They don't really want God at all. They want to come to God on their terms only and so are never satisfied—and they never will be satisfied.

I like bread. My wife has a cookbook that features 250 different kinds of breads. But there are thousands and thousands of different kinds of bread. My wife's favorite bread is sourdough.

My favorite bread is something called *nan*, which is made in India. It's good stuff. God knows the kind of bread you like and the kind of bread you need.

One of the things that thrills me about following the Lord is that he treats us as individuals. He doesn't deal with us all the same way. He knows what we need. He sees us as individuals. In your DNA, there is enough information to fill thousands of pages with information about how unique you really are. God knows all about your uniqueness, and when he deals with you, he treats you differently from the way he treats me. He custom designs a unique plan for each of us.

Jesus knows today whether you need the bread of love, the bread of mercy. He sees your pain and grief and realizes you need the bread of his compassion. He sees your longing for acceptance from others and knows whether you need the bread of acceptance. He knows your struggle to forgive yourself, so he sends the bread of his pardon. Jesus knows if you need the bread of motivation because you need a jump start in your life. He is aware of the mountains of adversity in your life that are too tall for you to cross, and he grants you the bread of faith. He knows your hopelessness and feeds you the bread of hope.

Jesus knows the bread that you need, and he is uniquely qualified to give you that bread. I can't offer it. Your spouse can't give it to you. Your friends can't give it to you. Only Jesus can satisfy your soul. Jesus stepped onto the scene and said, "Listen, your forefathers gave you this kind of bread, and they still died. But the bread I give to you is bread that will cause you to live forever. It will be bread that satisfies your soul."

The Bread of Life Strengthens Us

I have come to the realization that I'm at times too strong. My wife wants me to be strong. My kids want me to be strong. We admire strong and competent people. I want to be strong. But as long as I find strength in myself, I don't get to experience God's strength. In 2 Corinthians 12:9, Paul quoted Jesus, "My grace is sufficient for you, for my power is made perfect in weakness."

Paul then wrote, "Therefore I will boast all the more gladly about my weaknesses, so that Christ's power may rest on me. That is why, for Christ's sake, I delight in weaknesses, in insults, in hardships, in persecutions, in difficulties. For when I am weak, then I am strong" (vv. 9–10).

I find that the more control I try to exert on my life, the less control I really have. The more I surrender, the more under control my life really is—God's control. It doesn't mean that we're passionless or that we don't try to do anything. It just means we recognize we can trust him, that he provides the physical, mental, emotional, and spiritual abilities to navigate life. We say, "God, I trust you. Give me your strength."

The Bread of Life gives us the strength to say, "I don't have it all together. I'm not the person you always see." Jesus gives us the strength to be real and say, "Lord, I'm not strong. I need your strength."

Dan Clark, in the book *Chicken Soup for the Soul*, tells the story of a young boy who saw a sign at a pet shop that said "Puppies for Sale." He went in and asked how much the puppies are. The store owner told him they were $30–$50.

The little boy checked his pocket. "I have $2.37," he said. "Can I please look at them?" The store owner showed him the dogs, and one particular puppy caught the boy's attention. He was limping behind the others. "That's the little puppy I want to buy," he said.

"No, you don't want to buy that little dog," the store owner replied. "If you really want him, I'll just give him to you."

The little boy got quite upset and said, "No, that little dog is worth every bit as much as all the other dogs, and I'll pay full price. I'll give you $2.37 now, and 50 cents a month until I have him paid for."

The owner replied, "He is never going to be able to jump and play with you like the other puppies."

The boy reached down and pulled up his pant leg to show his badly crippled leg, supported by a metal brace. He said softly, "Well, I don't run so well myself, and the little puppy will need someone who understands."[4]

As I read that story, I thought, *I'm sure glad the Lord didn't wait for me to become perfect before he decided to love me, accept me, use me.* We all walk with a limp, and in our weakness we embrace his strength and say, "Lord, I need you. I am desperate for you. I want you in my life."

Some of us are still hungry because we choose to be. Jesus has made it clear. "If you come to me and you receive me, not only as your Savior and Lord, but as your friend, as your guide, I will satisfy your life, and I will strengthen your life." Most of us, however, haven't yet become desperate enough. We're just not hungry enough yet. We're still self-satisfied. We need to turn to Jesus, who satisfies our hunger and fills us completely.

> *Lord, move us to the point in life where we come to Jesus not for the gifts he gives, not to receive some hoped-for miracle, but because we realize he is the Bread of Life who saves, satisfies, and strengthens. Then our joy will be full. Help us find our rest in you.*

Application

1. "Some people have never been desperate for God. They don't know what it's like really to hunger for him." Have you ever desperately hungered for God? How has he filled you?

2. "Life is full of temporary fixes." To what "temporary fixes" and material things do you turn to fill your hunger? How can you learn to let Jesus satisfy your needs instead of trying to be self-sufficient?

3. "When you wake up on Sunday morning and you think about going to church, enjoying the music and the worship, I pray that you think, *I'm going to meet with God.*" What is your motivation for going to church? Are you eager to truly meet with and worship the Lord?

4. "Jesus knows today whether you need the bread of love, the bread of mercy. He sees your pain and grief and realizes you need the bread of his compassion." What kind of bread do you need from the Lord today?

5. "I find that the more control I try to exert on my life, the less control I really have. The more I surrender, the more under control my life really is—God's control." What things do you need to surrender to the Lord's control?

JESUS, OUR SHEPHERD

CHAPTER 7

THE GATE FOR THE SHEEP

*I AM THE GATE FOR THE SHEEP. ALL THOSE OTHERS ARE
UP TO NO GOOD—SHEEP STEALERS, EVERY ONE OF THEM.
BUT THE SHEEP DIDN'T LISTEN TO THEM. I AM THE GATE.
ANYONE WHO GOES THROUGH ME WILL BE CARED FOR—WILL
FREELY GO IN AND OUT, AND FIND PASTURE. A THIEF
IS ONLY THERE TO STEAL AND KILL AND DESTROY.
I CAME SO THEY CAN HAVE REAL AND ETERNAL LIFE, MORE
AND BETTER LIFE THAN THEY EVER DREAMED OF.*

—JOHN 10:7–10 MSG

I magine you have the ability to transport yourself through space faster than the speed of light. Some scientists are researching the possibilities of wormholes, a form of a black hole that connects distant parts of the universe.

These scientists think that, at some point in the future, people are actually going to be able to transport themselves through the universe via these wormholes. In the movie *Contact*,

Jodie Foster plays a scientist who, at the climax of the movie, transports herself from one part of the galaxy to another. Even though she goes far out into the universe and back again, she's only gone for half of a second. It's mind-boggling.

I saw another movie several years ago called *Stargate*, in which archaeologists find a gate in the desert. A scientist deciphers the writing on the gate and figures out how to go through the gate, which leads to a wormhole, which emerges on the other side of the galaxy.

This passage doesn't talk about a "stargate" or a wormhole. It's the "God Gate." It is a gate that leads to something even more spectacular than another galaxy!

Jesus in John 10 makes the incredible claim that he is the Gate—not just *a* gate, but *the* Gate, the one and only gate to God. He introduces his claim with a picture that should have been familiar to his listeners.

"I tell you the truth, the man who does not enter the sheep pen by the gate, but climbs in by some other way, is a thief and a robber. The man who enters by the gate is the shepherd of his sheep. The watchman opens the gate for him, and the sheep listen to his voice. He calls his own sheep by name and leads them out. When he has brought out all his own, he goes on ahead of them, and his sheep follow him because they know his voice. But they will never follow a stranger; in fact, they will run away from him because they do not recognize a stranger's voice."

Jesus used this figure of speech, but they did not understand what he was telling them. Therefore Jesus said again,

"I tell you the truth, I am the gate for the sheep. All who ever came before me were thieves and robbers, but the sheep did not listen to them. I am the gate; whoever enters through me will be saved. He will come in and go out, and find pasture. The thief comes only to steal and kill and destroy; I

have come that they may have life, and have it to
the full." (vv. 1–10)

This passage of Scripture, in which Jesus uses the allegory of
himself being the Shepherd and the Gate, gives us great hope
and great comfort. Several places in the Bible refer to God as a
Shepherd. One we often think of is the Twenty-third Psalm,
which begins, "The LORD is my shepherd." Psalm 100:3 says,
"We are his people, the sheep of his pasture." Isaiah wrote, "He
tends his flocks like a shepherd: He gathers the lambs in his
arms and carries them close to his heart; he gently leads those
that have young" (40:11).

Mark describes the people who followed Jesus as "sheep with-
out a shepherd" (6:34). Hebrews 13:20 speaks of Jesus as the
Great Shepherd. First Peter 5:4 calls him the Chief Shepherd. And
Jesus describes himself in John 10 as both a shepherd and a gate.

The God Gate

What was Jesus' motive for giving this discourse about
sheep and shepherds? We need to look at the context the pre-
ceding chapter provides. John 9 describes the encounter
between Jesus and a blind man. He had been born blind, yet
Jesus simply spit into the dirt on the ground, made a little mud
to put over the man's eyes, and miraculously healed him.

When the Pharisees heard about it, they were irate because
Jesus had healed the blind man on the Sabbath, which was
against their rules. The story continues with a dialogue between
the former blind man and the religious Pharisees.

First, the Pharisees talked to the man's parents, but the
parents just said, "Hey, what are you asking us for? He's an
adult; he can tell you what happened." So they ask him.
Despite the man's explanation, however, the Pharisees kick
him out of the synagogue.

Jesus knew the hearts of the leaders, and as he referred to himself as the Gate for the sheep, he was probably thinking back to the harshness of those Pharisees who would not accept the healing of the blind man. They certainly weren't happy he was healed. They certainly weren't praising the Lord.

I had an operation on my ear a few years ago to help improve my hearing. Afterward I was ecstatic. I could hear perfectly again! So I can kind of relate to this guy. I can see him running around, shouting, "I can see! I can see!"

But the Pharisees just blow him off. "Ah, who cares if you can see? Who healed you? We want to know who did this. Where is he?"

Jesus had those religious leaders in mind when he explained that the other shepherds were just thieves and robbers. He contrasted himself to them, saying, "I am the good shepherd" (John 10:11). He next describes himself as the Gate.

When I was in Wales, I had the opportunity to observe some sheep roaming on the beautiful hillsides. The sheep pens there were different from the ones you find in America. They were just little round areas with rocks stacked on top of each other. The shepherd would lead the sheep into these little pens. At night, the shepherd would lie down to sleep at the small opening that the sheep had entered. He became the door, or the gate.

Jesus addresses the crowd, which probably included some of the religious leaders, saying, "I am the Gate. I am the true Shepherd. I am the one who will bring you to God." What an incredible claim! And Jesus is the only one who could legitimately say it.

I recall from my college years a classic C. S. Lewis quote about Jesus.

> A man who was merely a man and said the sort of
> things Jesus said would not be a great moral teacher.

He would either be a lunatic—on the level with a man who says he's a poached egg—or else he'd be the Devil of Hell. You must make your choice. Either this man was, and is, the Son of God: or else a madman or something worse.[1]

When Jesus said, "I am the gate" (John 10:7), he claimed to be the only way, the only gate that leads to God.

The Only Gate

Lee Strobel, in his book *The Case for Christ*, describes an interview with Pastor Louis Lapides, a man whose background I found intriguing. Louis grew up in a conservative Jewish family, and although he went with his family to the synagogue, it never really affected their daily life. They never talked about the Bible at home, and the Messiah was never mentioned. Louis's only impressions of Jesus were pictures of him in the windows of Catholic churches. He didn't even realize Jesus had any connection to the Jews!

When Louis was seventeen, his parents divorced, and he began to reject even the little religious upbringing he had. "What good is religion if it can't help people in a practical way?" he wondered. "I didn't feel as if I had a personal relationship with God. I had a lot of beautiful ceremonies and traditions, but he was the distant and detached God of Mount Sinai who said, 'Here are the rules—you live by them, you'll be okay; and I'll see you later.'"

After his parents' divorce, Louis went through a time of rebellion. He eventually was drafted into the army and served in Vietnam. There in 1967 on his first assignment, he came into contact with things he'd never seen before—bodies blown apart and all the other horrible atrocities of war. His assignment was to guard a boat filled with ammunition, so he figured he was a "sitting duck" if something ever came down their way, and he felt a little nervous about it.

Louis began picking up books on Eastern religions and started reading about Buddhism, Hinduism, and various religious things, trying to find something that would mean something to him. He said, "I was extremely bothered by the evil I had seen, and I was trying to figure out how faith can deal with it. I used to say, 'If there is a God, I don't care if I find him on Mount Sinai or Mount Fuji. I'll take him either way.'"

He returned from Vietnam with a taste for marijuana and plans to become a Buddhist priest. He tried to find God by being a Buddhist priest but quickly realized he could never be good enough for God. He became depressed and began to consider ending his own life. He started using harder drugs until he finally decided to make a clean break, and he moved to Los Angeles to start his life over again.

There, too, Louis jumped from spiritual experiment to spiritual experiment. He tried to find God in Chinese Buddhism, Japanese Buddhism, Hinduism, and Scientology. He even dabbled in satanic worship.

In 1969, Louis went down to Sunset Strip to gawk at an evangelist there who had chained himself to an eight-foot cross in a protest. There he encountered some Christians who engaged him in a debate. First, he threw some Eastern philosophy at them. "There is no one God out there. We're god. I'm god. You're god. You just have to realize it."

One person asked him, "Well, if you're god, why don't you create a rock?" Louis was pretty stoned at the time, so he just held out his empty hand and said, "Yeah, well, here's a rock." The Christian replied, "That's the difference between you and the true God. When God creates something, everyone can see it. It's objective, not subjective." That struck Louis. He decided if he was going to find God, he would have to be objectively true.

As he continued the conversation, the name of Jesus came up. One of the Christians asked him, "Do you know of the prophecies about the Messiah?" Louis had no idea. A pastor started talking about some of the Old Testament prophecies.

Louis suddenly realized the man was talking about his Jewish Scriptures! What could they have to do with Jesus? The pastor offered him a Bible and encouraged him to go home and ask the God of Abraham, Isaac, and Jacob to show him if Jesus was the Messiah.

Louis started to read in Genesis and found he couldn't put that Old Testament down because he started reading things that really bothered him. When he came to the fifty-third chapter of Isaiah, his blood went cold. Right there, Isaiah mapped out the life and times of the Messiah, and he immediately recognized Jesus. He thought the Bible had been rigged. He thought, *Oh, the guy gave me a fake Bible,* so he had his stepmother send him a Jewish Bible. But it said the same thing!

While he sat in his room one day, Louis considered opening up the New Testament. He decided to read just one page. He turned to the first page in the New Testament—Matthew's genealogy—and was shocked because even there in the genealogies he began to see and understand who Jesus was.

Louis realized he needed to do something about Jesus. So he went out for a spiritual retreat under the desert sky, and he prayed, "God, I've got to come to the end of this struggle. I have to know beyond a shadow of a doubt that Jesus is the Messiah." There, out in the desert, he accepted Jesus Christ into his heart. He admitted that his life was a mess, and he cried out to Jesus to save him.

He went from there to college and, eventually, to seminary. Louis has since taught at Talbot Seminary and has been a teacher for Walk Thru the Bible Ministries. He and his wife lead a ministry called Beth Ariel Fellowship in Sherman Oaks, California.

As Lee Strobel interviewed Louis, he asked him about the prophecies that Jesus fulfilled, posing to him the most common objections. Couldn't Jesus have fulfilled the prophecies merely by accident?

Louis responded, "The odds are so astronomical that they rule that out.... The probability of just eight prophecies being fulfilled is one chance in one hundred million billion!" The odds are the same as if you covered the whole state of Texas in silver dollars two feet deep (that would be one hundred million billion silver dollars) and sent a man in blindfolded to pick out one particular specially marked coin. What are the odds he would choose the right one? The same as the odds that one man would fulfill just eight of the prophecies Jesus did.

And yet, Jesus fulfilled forty-eight prophecies! What would the odds of that be? One chance in a trillion, trillion, trillion, trillion, trillion, trillion, trillion, trillion, trillion, trillion, trillion, trillion, trillion!

Strobel explored another objection to Jesus' identity. Perhaps Jesus intentionally structured his life in order to make his life match the Old Testament prophecies, making choices that ensured those things happened to him. He might have been able to accomplish that for a couple of them, Louis admits. But what do you do when the Old Testament Scriptures prophesied exactly where you're to be born, your ancestry, your method of execution, and the fact that thirty pieces of silver would be given in exchange for your life? It just doesn't work.

All of these amazing statistics about fulfillment of prophecy caused Louis to realize that Jesus really was the Messiah.[2]

Jesus is the God Gate. He said, "There is no other way to God except through me." I love the scene in *Stargate* in which the characters pass through the gate into the wormhole. They emerge a split second later on the other side of the universe. That, in a sense, is what happened to Louis. Louis was out in a desert, not knowing exactly what to say. All he did was to cry out, "God, I've made a mess of my life, and I need you to clean it up." At that moment he went through the God Gate, and in a split second he was with God and God was with him.

When you leave a building and go out through the door, you enter another place. We don't even consciously think about it. We enter and exit places all day long. It is a seamless transition for us. It is also a seamless transition when we come to Jesus and say, "Be my Gate." There are no fireworks Just an instantaneous change that accompanies a surrender that says, "God, here I am. I've made a mess and I need you. Come into my life."

Have you entered through the God Gate? Jesus is the only one who can lead us to the Father. All others who claim to know the way are thieves and robbers who come to kill and steal and destroy. We must put our faith in Christ and no one else, because he is the Great Shepherd who cares immensely for his sheep. He died to save us, and he now lives as the Gate to the heavenly Father.

> *Thank you, Jesus, for being the God Gate and our true Shepherd. Help us not to wander, but to follow you closely and listen for your voice. We don't want to be led astray by false shepherds. Guide us and protect us while we journey on earth.*

Application

1. "Jesus uses the allegory of himself being the Shepherd and the Gate, [which] gives us great hope and great comfort." How does the picture of Jesus as the Shepherd and the Gate give you comfort and hope? What worries can you lay down as you remember Jesus is taking care of you and protecting you?
2. "Louis realized he needed to do something about Jesus." What evidence about the claims of Jesus calls you to a place of decision for Christ?

3. "Louis was out in a desert, not knowing exactly what to say. All he did was to cry out, 'God, I've made a mess of my life, and I need you to clean it up.' At that moment he went through the God Gate, and in a split second he was with God and God was with him." Take some time to reflect on your own experience of entry through the God Gate. How has having Jesus as your Shepherd affected you?

4. "Jesus is the only one who can lead us to the Father. All others who claim to know the way are thieves and robbers who come to kill and steal and destroy." What "others" have tried to lead you astray from God's flock?

CHAPTER 8

THE GOOD SHEPHERD

I AM THE GOOD SHEPHERD. THE GOOD SHEPHERD PUTS THE
SHEEP BEFORE HIMSELF, SACRIFICES HIMSELF IF NECESSARY. A
HIRED MAN IS NOT A REAL SHEPHERD. THE SHEEP MEAN NOTHING
TO HIM. HE SEES A WOLF COME AND RUNS FOR IT, LEAVING THE
SHEEP TO BE RAVAGED AND SCATTERED BY THE WOLF. HE'S ONLY
IN IT FOR THE MONEY. THE SHEEP DON'T MATTER TO HIM.

I AM THE GOOD SHEPHERD. I KNOW MY OWN SHEEP
AND MY OWN SHEEP KNOW ME. IN THE SAME WAY,
THE FATHER KNOWS ME AND I KNOW THE FATHER.

—JOHN 10:11–15 MSG

A shepherd was herding his flock in a remote pasture when a man drove up in a brand-new Jeep Cherokee. He wore a fancy suit and a stylish tie. As he rolled down his window, he looked at the shepherd and asked, "Now, if I can tell you how many sheep you have out here, will you give me one?"

The shepherd thought, *Well, that's kind of interesting.* "Sure, if you can figure out how many sheep I've got out here, I'll give you one."

So the guy in the fancy suit took out his cell phone and a small computer, hooked up the cell phone to the computer, and dialed into a global positioning satellite up in the sky. He downloaded some files and opened up some different things in his computer and finally printed out a 140-page report. "You have 1,586 sheep."

The shepherd had to admit, "Man, you're right. You can have one." So the guy walked over to the little flock, picked up a sheep, and put it in his car.

But before he could take off, the shepherd said, "Now, wait a minute. If I can tell you what you do for a living, will you give the sheep back to me?"

The guy thought, *Well, that's a good challenge.* He agreed, "Yeah, I'll do that. What do I do for a living?"

"You're a consultant."

"How did you know I'm a consultant?" the guy asked.

The shepherd replied, "Oh, that's easy. You turn up here without being asked, you want to be paid for information I already knew, and you still don't know anything about my business because you just took off with my sheep dog."

Shepherds are attuned to the condition and the needs of their sheep; and Jesus, the Good Shepherd, knows his sheep intimately. He explains in John 10 his role as the Good Shepherd. His sheep know his voice and follow him. He cares for, protects, and willingly lays down his life for his sheep.

In the last chapter we looked at how the Pharisees reacted to the healing of the blind man in John 9. They were upset with Jesus for healing on the Sabbath, and they gave no glory to God. They weren't excited at all that this man had been miraculously healed! Their only concern was that Jesus had broken one of their little man-made laws. The context sets the stage for Jesus to introduce himself as the Good Shepherd—one who sacrifices for the sheep and cares for them, unlike the Pharisees.

Jesus points out the difference between the Good Shepherd and others who try to lead the sheep astray. He calls them strangers, robbers and thieves, and hired hands. Let's take a look at each of these "false shepherds."

Strangers

Jesus often uses characters in place of names or groups of people in a story, and we need to understand the analogy he makes. "Sheep" refers to the Jewish people. He says in verse 16, "I have other sheep that are not of this sheep pen. I must bring them also. They too will listen to my voice, and there shall be one flock and one shepherd." The "other" sheep are the people of non-Jewish descent who will come to Jesus as well.

When Jesus talks about the strangers, thieves and robbers, and hired hands, he is referring to the Pharisees. They were supposed to lead the way spiritually for Israel, but clearly they weren't doing a good job of it.

"They will never follow a stranger; in fact, they will run away from him because they do not recognize a stranger's voice" (John 10:5). The Pharisees, one of the prominent religious groups at the time, often cared more about their petty rules and regulations than they cared about God. They frequently placed the enforcement of man-made traditions above the needs of the people. That explains why Jesus so often talked about them and responded to them with such distaste. *How* you did something mattered more to them than your motive and purpose for doing it. They maintained and enforced a system of religious bondage in the lives of their people.

Because the Pharisees were more interested in human's approval than God's approval, their whole world revolved around their ability to impress other people with their false piety. They held their heads high with a sanctimonious air that set them apart from the common Jew. But in their hearts there was no true love for God. For them religious devotion was just a performance.

As spiritual leaders, the Pharisees were about as useful to their fellow Jews as a stranger is to a flock of sheep. But Jesus was the Good Shepherd. He came to give his life to save the sheep. Jesus points out that the sheep recognize his voice; they *know* it. He uses the word "know" several times in this passage, and it is a key word. It does not mean simply intellectual knowledge or information. It means to "experientially know." It is a knowledge based on a relationship. Jesus says, "My sheep know my voice because they walk with me—because I lead them and guide them and they trust me."

Jesus uses the same word for "know" in Matthew 7:21–23, where he says,

> Not everyone who says to me, "Lord, Lord," will enter the kingdom of heaven, but only he who does the will of my Father who is in heaven. Many will say to me on that day, "Lord, Lord, did we not prophesy in your name, and in your name drive out demons and perform many miracles?" Then I will tell them plainly, "I never knew you."

Jesus certainly was *aware* of those people, but he never *knew* them. They did not have a *relationship* with Jesus. Neither did the Pharisees *know* God. Their spirituality was all traditions, rules, and rituals. There was no relationship.

The Pharisees had it all figured out—what to do, how to talk, and how to behave. Yet they never truly experienced God. It's a great question for us: Do we know God experientially?

When we know God, we learn to recognize his voice. I recently spoke with a woman in our church who took a vacation to visit the Holy Land. She described the way the sheep would graze in a large group out in the countryside. It was a communal group, with several shepherds keeping watch. For various reasons, including safety, they let the flocks mingle together, so the sheep get pretty mixed up. But as my friend Helen watched, one of the shepherds began to call to his sheep; and, one by one, sheep from different parts of the flock began to come toward him. Another shepherd called out, and other sheep began to migrate toward him. The sheep knew the voice of their shepherd.

Shepherds in Israel have called their sheep in this way since biblical times. The Jews of Jesus' day knew what it meant when Jesus said, "My sheep listen to my voice; I know them, and they follow me" (John 10:27).

God knows your name. Jesus calls you by name. Isn't that amazing? He called his disciples by name as he said, "Come, follow me," and he still calls us to be his followers. When you hear your name, what do you think? What goes through your mind?

People call your name every day. They call you on the phone, write you an e-mail, greet you in the hall, or call you when you sit in a waiting room. People use your name all the time. It's likely, however, that many of the people who call your name know little about you. You may be just a name on a list. They have no personal firsthand knowledge of you. But when Jesus calls your name, he knows everything about you. You are more to him than just a name on a list. You are a unique person, whom he has chosen to be one of his sheep.

Is Jesus a stranger to you? When he calls your name, does it sound like a doctor's receptionist who calls out your name but doesn't know you? Or does it sound like the familiar voice of a dear friend who calls you on the phone? I pray that you listen carefully for his voice, that you recognize him as the Good Shepherd, and that you don't listen to the voices of the stranger who wants to lead you astray.

Thieves and Robbers

Jesus next contrasts himself with those who want to hurt the sheep—the thieves and robbers. Jesus lumps them together because thieves and robbers violate both your *property* and your *person*. Jesus says in John 10:10, "These guys are coming into the sheep pen and stealing the sheep. They're taking sheep that do not belong to them" (author's paraphrase). If you've ever experienced a break-in at your house, or been held up by an armed robber, you felt *violated*. That's what the Pharisees did. They violated people with the six hundred man-made laws they used to control people. They used guilt and intimidation to pressure people to look and act the same.

I have a friend who was once pastor of my church. He shared with our congregation the following story as an example of misjudging people:

> Her hair was green that Sunday morning in church. One of the tenors peeked at her from the choir room before they entered. Each week several choir members had a friendly bet going on as to which color her hair would be. It was often blue but sometimes it turned between purple and green. An alto won the bet that Sunday. It was green.
>
> In our former community, I sometimes heard remarks about that girl with the weirdly colored hair. She clearly stood out in the conservative community of Prescott, Arizona. A dental assistant cleaning my teeth talked about the strange girl with the two-tone hairstyle, green at the ends and bleach blonde on top. She wondered about the girl's family. Was she a troubled kid looking for attention at the high school? The assistant was sure this girl probably used drugs. One thing for sure, she wanted her son to stay away from that girl.

When she talked to my friend and pastor that day, the dental assistant didn't know that girl came to his church or who she was. At the end of the pastor's message on misjudging people, he said, "By the way, remember that girl with the green hair in church? That was my daughter."

Pharisees always wanted the people to look and act the same as they did. Anything different was considered "unholy." They thought that God judged what was on the outside, just like the dental assistant who judged the appearance of my friend's daughter. But God looks at the heart.

Jesus called the Pharisees thieves because they were stealing the joy and life from the people they were supposed to love and protect. They really didn't love them at all.

We still have thieves and robbers today who pass themselves off as shepherds. There are pastors who are thieves; they steal the joy of their people through manipulation and intimidation, making the Bible say things that it doesn't really say. They choose the law over the Spirit. They choose the bondage of legalism over freedom in Christ.

In Zechariah 11, God called those kinds of shepherds "worthless shepherd[s]." Why? Because they stole the joy of the people. They robbed the people of the experience of knowing God. For them, form was more important than the Spirit of God.

Paul wrote in Romans 5:6–8, "You see, at just the right time, when we were still powerless, Christ died for the ungodly. Very rarely will anyone die for a righteous man, though for a good man someone might possibly dare to die. But God demonstrates his own love for us in this: While we were still sinners, Christ died for us." Jesus knows what our ungodliness looks like. He knows your name, and he also knows your nature.

Perhaps you say, "No one really understands me. I wish someone would know me well enough to understand me." I'm not sure we'll ever find someone on this earth who will know us well enough to truly understand us. But Jesus does. And Jesus says, "I am the Good Shepherd, and I call my sheep by name, and I know my sheep." He knows your *name*, and he knows *you*.

Jesus demonstrates his intimate knowledge of his sheep through his interactions with the twelve disciples. He knew how to work with each of them. They had different natures. They came from different situations and backgrounds. Jesus took them as individuals and worked with their personalities, their passions, their interests, their temperaments, their strengths, and their weaknesses. He knew when to be blunt with hotheaded Peter (Matt. 16:23), when to be gentle with John (John 19:26–27), and he anticipated what each disciple needed.

Just as he knew how to work with each of his disciples, Jesus knows how to work with you. He works with you as an individual, because you are his and he knows you by name. He knows your nature and what it will take to mold you. The way he molds you is not going to be the same as the way he molds me. I love to see the way God works in people's lives. And I think, *Wow, he knows exactly what they need.*

Jesus says, "Listen, I'm the Good Shepherd. I own the sheep, and I lay down my life for the sheep. I love those sheep." If you are one of his, he is your Shepherd, and nothing you do will make the Shepherd love you any more or less. You can't read your Bible more, pray more, or give more and by doing so increase his love for you. He will never love you more than he does at this moment. God may bless us according to what we do, but it doesn't change his love for us. He is the Good Shepherd, and we have all of his love simply because he chooses to love us.

We should still serve God. We should still give. We should still be active in the church. But we don't do these things to earn God's love. We listen to his voice, serve him, and follow him because he has proved himself to be our reliable and trustworthy Shepherd who will lead us to green pastures.

Hired Hand

Another kind of false shepherd is the *hired hand*. He may know who the sheep are, but he doesn't know what they need. Jesus, the Good Shepherd, not only knows our names and our nature but also our exact needs.

Hired hands are like rent-a-shepherds. They have no real interest in the sheep. The only reason they watch the sheep is because they want some cash. They are the ones who think, *Oh, this is a great job. We'll just kind of lay around all day, listen to our iPods, kind of watch the sheep, and they'll pay us.* But they have no real concern for the sheep.

Jesus tells us, "Those shepherds are not going to be there for you." The law in biblical times required a hired hand to defend the sheep if one wolf attacked the sheep. If two wolves attacked, they could run. Real shepherds, however, would stay and defend the sheep, no matter what. It was the hired hands who would quickly bail.

The people knew hired hands didn't care about the sheep, so they understood exactly what Jesus meant. A shepherd who is not the real shepherd isn't interested in your needs or your protection or where you are at this point in your life. He doesn't care.

I think Jesus was probably thinking back to the blind man he healed. The Pharisees, those false shepherds, didn't care that the blind man could now see. They didn't care about people at all. Only appearances. But Jesus came along saying, "I am the Good Shepherd, and I care. I care about you and about your needs."

Sheep are pretty helpless creatures. If one falls on its back, it will often just lay there like a turtle because it can't even roll back over onto its feet. Sheep will munch on a poisonous plant, because they don't know the difference. That's why the shepherd's role is so crucial. The shepherd is always there to move them away from the toxic plants and to help them back on their feet when they fall. He knows them; he is interested in their needs and takes care of them. Jesus says, "I am the Good Shepherd. I know your needs."

People have a lot of needs. We have physical needs like food, clothing, and shelter. We have emotional needs for love and support. We have spiritual needs. I am so grateful it's not up to me to take care of everyone's needs. Instead, we have a Good Shepherd who knows the needs of each person and who is ready and able to provide for them.

The greatest need you have today is not for a new relationship or job. It's not for some new plaything to fill up your time. The greatest need you have is constant communion with God. That's one of the reasons going to church to meet with God is so important. We gather to meet and to worship him, to have him fill our hearts. The shepherd calls his sheep, they recognize his voice, and they get up and move.

When I was a kid, I used to irritate my parents because they would ask me to do things, and I would use the typical line, "Just a minute." I was really consistent with that response. But "just a minute" generally meant a lot longer than a minute. I could never figure out why that irritated my dad so much. Now, I have three boys of my own. When I ask them to do something, I inevitably get the same response, "Just a minute."

What do you mean "just a minute"? What we want them to say is, "Oh yes, Dad, you're the greatest father in the whole world, and I would like to do anything that you ask me to do, because you're so rich in mercy and grace, and you pay for everything that I have, and you give me food to eat. You're so wonderful, Dad. I'll be right there."

Maybe it's because we parents know what we do for our kids. They're not going to figure it out until they have kids of their own. They'll wake up someday and realize, "Wow, my parents did a lot for me. Dad wasn't so bad after all."

We do a lot for our kids. Sometimes we say to them, "I need a little help here for just a second. Could you come help me?" At those moments, "just a minute" isn't quite the response we're looking for.

Jesus calls you by name. Could you imagine what it would have been like for him to walk by and say, "Matthew, come, follow me," and have Matthew reply, "Just a minute, Lord"?

Or what if Jesus came by and said, "Zacchaeus, come down out of that tree; I'm going to stay with you today," and Zacchaeus replied, "Give me a second, would ya?"

Jesus calls you by name today and says, "Follow me. Let me have your life. Let me be Lord of your life." Will your response be, "Just a minute, Lord"? I wonder if the Lord feels the same way we do when our kids give us that response.

The Lord whispers, "Listen, I am the Good Shepherd. I know your name. I know everything about you. I know your nature. I know the ugliness that is in your life, and I still love you. I know your needs more than you yourself know your needs. If you follow me and give up this battle with me, I can lead you better than you can lead yourself."

Our response should not be, "Just a minute." It should be, "Yes, Lord!"

I received an e-mail from a man who had read my book *In God We Trust, but Only as a Last Resort*. His life changed because he finally realized that he had to make a decision. Either he had to let the Good Shepherd totally lead, or he had to refuse his leadership altogether. There could be no middle ground.

The Good Shepherd says to us, "I lay down my life for my sheep. I lay down my life for those whom the Father has given me. Don't listen to the false shepherds, the ones who care only about themselves and lead my sheep astray. Follow me, and I will take care of you."

The Good Shepherd is calling you by name today. He knows your voice. Do you recognize his?

Lord, help us to recognize the voice of our Good Shepherd. Make us open and available as you speak to us, as you minister to us, as you whisper peace into our hearts. We

want to be open to your leadership, because only you can
keep us safe and provide for every need.

Application

1. "They frequently placed the enforcement of man-
   made traditions above the needs of the people....
   They maintained and enforced a system of religious
   bondage in the lives of their people." What spiritual rules and traditions do you impose on yourself
   and others? How can you find freedom from the
   bondage of legalism by following Jesus' voice?
2. "Jesus says, 'My sheep know my voice because they
   walk with me—because I lead them and guide them
   and they trust me.'" Do you walk closely with
   Jesus? How do you hear his voice and see his guid-
   ance in your life?
3. "Perhaps you say, 'No one really understands me. I
   wish someone would know me well enough to
   understand me.' ... But Jesus does." Do you find
   comfort in the knowledge that Jesus always understands you and can see things from your
   perspective? How does this change the way you
   approach daily life?
4. "He works with you as an individual, because you
   are his and he knows you by name. He knows your
   nature and what it will take to mold you." In what
   ways is Jesus molding you today? Are you allowing
   him to work in your heart and life?
5. "The shepherd's role is so crucial. The shepherd is
   always there to move [the sheep] away from the
   toxic plants and to help them back on their feet
   when they fall." How has Jesus protected you and
   helped you back on your feet? Has the experience
   of his care helped you trust him more?

JESUS, OUR DIRECTION

CHAPTER 9

THE WAY

"DON'T LET THIS THROW YOU. YOU TRUST GOD, DON'T YOU? TRUST ME. THERE IS PLENTY OF ROOM FOR YOU IN MY FATHER'S HOME. IF THAT WEREN'T SO, WOULD I HAVE TOLD YOU THAT I'M ON MY WAY TO GET A ROOM READY FOR YOU? AND IF I'M ON MY WAY TO GET YOUR ROOM READY, I'LL COME BACK AND GET YOU SO YOU CAN LIVE WHERE I LIVE. AND YOU ALREADY KNOW THE ROAD I'M TAKING."

THOMAS SAID, "MASTER, WE HAVE NO IDEA WHERE YOU'RE GOING. HOW DO YOU EXPECT US TO KNOW THE ROAD?"

JESUS SAID, "I AM THE ROAD, ALSO THE TRUTH, ALSO THE LIFE. NO ONE GETS TO THE FATHER APART FROM ME."

—JOHN 14:1–6 MSG

There are many people in our world today who think they know the way to God.

Some people claim the way to God is through enlightenment

or through doing good works. A few cults even believe they can get to God by killing themselves.

Jesus makes a bold claim when he claims to be the *only* way to the Father. Jesus explains to his disciples in John 14 how to find him in the future. He leaves a forwarding address. That's why we worship him. Our worship of Jesus is not just for the here and now; it's a worship that will last forever.

John 14:6 is one of the most frequently quoted and memorized verses in the Bible: "I am the way and the truth and the life. No one comes to the Father except through me." The *way*, the *truth*, and the *life*. Those three words contain so much meaning that they merit our focus for this entire section.

The disciples were concerned because Jesus had recently spoken about leaving them. So he comforts them by telling them that he is going to prepare a place for them and that he will come back again. It is a passage that we read often at memorial services and funerals because it gives us great hope. If the person who passed away was a follower of Jesus, we know we will have a joyful reunion someday in heaven.

Of course, Thomas was not satisfied. "Lord, we don't know the way," he said. The disciples were certainly upset. Jesus was going to leave them, and they wanted to know where he was going.

As I read that passage, I think that Jesus must have been a wonderful person to "hang out with." The disciples wanted to be with him, and not just because he could turn the water into wine or feed the multitudes from a couple of loaves and fish. They wanted to be in his presence.

I can't wait to get to heaven and hear about what it was like to spend time with Jesus here on earth. I wonder if he joked with his disciples. Perhaps he teased them a little bit. I wonder what it felt like to watch him do miracles.

Thomas expressed a concern that all the disciples felt at Jesus' statement. None of them wanted him to leave. But Thomas was the pessimistic one, always a little doubtful, and he was going to make sure he knew where Jesus was going. The look on his face must have been priceless as Jesus replied, "*I* am the way."

The Way Is an Offense

While the words of Jesus in the beginning of John 14 are full of hope, when we get to verse 6, they take a little turn. He goes from talking about mansions and rooms in his Father's house to a very select statement: "I am the way and the truth and the life. *No one* comes to the Father *except* through me." That's strong language, and it is offensive to many people.

In 2003, news correspondent Peter Arnett lost his job with CNN because of his critical statements about the military in Iraq. However true his statements may have been, they offended a lot of people. At about the same time, the singing group Dixie Chicks made some negative comments about President Bush and found themselves facing the disapproval of country music fans.

Words can be offensive. The words of Jesus have offended people for centuries, and they will continue to be offensive to those who choose not to face the truth. Many of Jesus' claims did not sit well with the leaders of the day. "I am the Bread of Life." "I am the Light of the World." "I am the resurrection." "I am the Good Shepherd." But John 14:6 may top them all. "I am the way.... No one comes to the Father except through me."

One of the biggest reasons his claim is so offensive is that it leaves them without a choice. We don't like being told that we have only one viable option. We are a country of consumers who like choices—many choices. We want choices about the cars we drive, the clothes we wear, the churches we attend, and on and on. With so many religions, each claiming to lead people to God, Christianity stands alone in its declaration: "There is only one option. There is only one way. Jesus is the way."

We Americans have choices in just about every area of life—airlines, cars, mortgage plans, restaurants, or marriage partners—and we like it that way. But Jesus says there's only one choice when it comes to how to get to heaven.

Some people will say, "Don't tell me how to find God. I will do it myself and in my own way. Don't tell me I have only one choice, because I will find God on my own. I'm smart enough. I can figure it out." The message of the cross is an offense, just as Paul wrote: "We preach Christ crucified: a stumbling block to Jews and foolishness to Gentiles" (1 Cor. 1:23).

Those words are hard, strong, and unbending. That should prompt a couple of responses from us. First, because the message can be offensive to unbelievers, we need to pray. We need to pray that the Lord will open their hearts to receive it. Second, we need to be careful *how* we say such things. We need to give the message, without diminishing the meaning, in a spirit of love. Otherwise it comes across as arrogant and obnoxious.

One of the tellers at my bank knows I'm a Christian, and she likes to bait me. Whenever I tell her she is doing a great job, she makes a snide comment to see what I'll do. I don't give her a speech on Christianity or "Genesis to Revelation in ninety seconds" or anything like that. But we are building a friendship, and I am planting spiritual seeds. She is used to aggressive, offensive Christians who bludgeon her with their message. I want her to know that I am not pressuring her.

When we witness to an unbeliever, it is so important to communicate in loving words. In fact, it is impossible to communicate the love of God in nonloving words. When we tell someone how wonderful it is to know Jesus Christ, and we share Jesus' words, "I am the way. There is no other way to the Father," it shouldn't be with an air of superiority. We don't have to shout. We don't have to push. All we need to do is calmly put it out there and let the Spirit of God do the rest. You and I can't bring anyone to the Lord. Only the Spirit of God can do that.

Mahatma Gandhi once said, speaking of Christianity, "I like their Christ. I don't like Christians." Why? Because he had observed a spirit of harshness and a spirit of arrogance. He waited to see the spirit of love that Jesus said we, as his followers, should have.

We cannot change the message that Jesus is the way. There will always be those who find it offensive. But we can present our message in a loving and kind way that demonstrates how Jesus desires everyone to find the way to the Father.

The Way Is Exclusive

Another hard truth for people to digest is the exclusive nature of Jesus' words. When I say, "Jesus is the way," to a group of Christians, they nod their heads and respond, "Oh yeah, that's a great passage, and I memorized that when I was young. Amen."

Imagine, though, that you're at an office lunch party enjoying some light and casual conversation. The topic of religion comes up. They know that you go to church and that you're a follower of Jesus. They ask you, "So what do you think?" You think for a minute, and you decide to quote John 14, verse 6: "I am the way and the truth and the life. No one comes to the Father except through me."

You will probably instantly hear words like "spiritual bigotry" or "religious chauvinism." People will say, "Oh, that's the thing about you Christians. You're so exclusive. You think you have the only way to God."

After traveling around this globe a few times, the one thing of which I remain convinced is that every religion on this planet is exclusive. Each one claims to have the truth, and anything contrary to its version of truth is error and therefore worthy of rejection.

We must be absolutely convinced of who Jesus was, who Jesus is, the reliability of the Bible, the credibility of the eyewitnesses, and the historical reality of the resurrection. We should study all the apologetic material we can get our hands on, because we need to be certain of the truth of Christianity. If we are to say Jesus is the only way, we must be ready to defend the trustworthiness of that statement.

Christianity is not based upon a principle, a creed, a philosophy, or even a book of scriptures. Christianity stands upon the person of Jesus Christ. Jesus is the sum total of Christianity. Jesus is a historical figure whom God sent to pay the price for our sin and to bring us into the relationship with God for which we have been longing and looking. Throughout the years, skeptics and critics from every age have tried to diminish Jesus' teachings, life, and resurrection. But Jesus continues to stand tall, and we must be convinced of that.

Jesus answers the greatest questions of all—questions regarding our origin, the meaning of life, morality, and our eternal destiny. Yes, we believe by faith, but that faith rests upon an insurmountable amount of evidence.

Ravi Zacharias, a great author and apologist, said, "A man rejects God neither because of intellectual demands nor because of the scarcity of evidence. A man rejects God because of moral resistance that refuses to admit his need for God."[1]

When asked why Christianity is not attractive to many people, Zacharias said,

> Buddhism and other religious systems basically tell people how to pull themselves up by their ethical bootstraps.... [Christ] calls you to die to yourself. Anytime truth involves a total commitment in which you bring yourself to complete humility, to the surrender of the will, you will always have resistance. Christ violates our power and our autonomy.[2]

People don't reject Christ because they have examined the evidence. They reject him because they really don't want to submit to his authority. In our human nature, we'd rather make it on our own. We'd prefer to pick and choose as we go along.

But Jesus says clearly, "I am the way. I am the only way. There is no other way." People will always ask the question, "Okay, then what about those people who have never heard about Jesus? What happens to them?" But the Bible is clear in its answer. We just have to venture outside of our theological box to allow God to answer this question.

In Acts 17:26–28, Paul said,

> From one man he made every nation of men, that they should inhabit the whole earth; and he determined the times set for them and the exact places where they should live. God did this so that men would seek him and perhaps reach out for him and find him, though he is not far from each one of us. "For in him we live and move and have our being."

He wrote in Romans 1:20, "For since the creation of the world God's invisible qualities—his eternal power and divine nature—have been clearly seen, being understood from what has been made, so that men are without excuse." God, through his creation, has made it very clear that he is present, involved, and available in this universe. We are not alone. I can look at the stars and say, "There must be a God," but how do I move from that revelation of nature to really knowing Jesus if I'm living far away from anyone who can tell me about him?

Let's never forget that God knows the heart of every man and woman, and he knows those who are truly seeking after him. After all, God is not some feeble god sitting powerless in a rocking chair who hopes some Christian will happen to stumble on a remote tribe and tell it about Jesus. He doesn't wipe his forehead and say, "Whew! I almost lost that group over there." No, that's not God. God is powerful. He is supernatural. God exceeds our ability to think or imagine. God can do whatever he wants to do. He can use any method he wants to get the complete salvation story into the minds and hearts of individuals.

Sadhu Sundar Singh was an Indian teacher and preacher who had an incredible testimony of how he came to the Lord. He prayed to God to reveal himself, and God gave him a vision of Jesus Christ. Skeptics scoffed, "Oh no, that couldn't happen." But he saw Jesus, and as a result he gave his heart to Jesus. Since then, God has used him to bring millions to Jesus Christ. God stepped outside of the box we like to put him in, and Jesus claimed this man's heart.

Most Muslims come to faith in one of two ways. They either meet a Christian and experience the love of Jesus through that person's life, which prompts them to accept Jesus Christ in their own lives, or Jesus reveals himself to them through dreams and visions. I have talked to Muslims in several countries and have heard many such stories.

When a person says, "Well, what do you do about those who haven't heard?" I leave it in God's hands. God has the power. He has the ability. God can use anything he wants to bring a person to faith in Jesus Christ.

Jesus said, "I am the way and the truth and the life. No one comes to the Father except through me." Those words are definitely offensive. They are exclusive. But the words of Jesus are also redemptive.

God created you for himself. He created you to know him. You will never be satisfied until you know him. How do we find God? We find him through his Son, Jesus, who died on the cross to pay the penalty for all of our junk, all of our sin, and to bring us into a new relationship with him.

Before the fall, Adam and Eve were in communion with God. They knew the truth, and they knew it came from God. They possessed life both physically and spiritually. After the fall, though, they experienced alienation from

God. They fell into falsehood and error, and they began to know death.

Then Jesus appeared, and the great news of Jesus in John 14:6 is that there is now a way back to God. There is truth instead of lies and errors, and there is life instead of death. Jesus came to make dead people live again. We need to say, "Lord, I bow before you. I recognize and admit that I need you, and I believe that Jesus died for me." Until that time comes, we're just bodies walking around, and there is no life. Jesus said, "I am the way. I am here to lead you back to God." Whether you're a cynic or a sympathizer, whether you're a person who loves church or despises it, until you meet the person of Jesus, you haven't found the way.

Facts are important. Study is important. Knowledge is important. But what is most important is that you and I have met Jesus, the Savior. Our faith may waiver at times. We may even at times seem to drift from the Lord. We may have doubts and questions. But when we truly come to that point in our life where we say, "Jesus, come into my life," we will know we've met the Savior. His Spirit will bear witness to our spirit that we are his.

Critics may laugh, family may not understand, and friends may think we're crazy, but once we've invited him into our lives, we can stand up against anything. We will know in our hearts that we are saved.

We have the best story in the world to tell. We have the most amazing message ever spoken. We are his messengers to tell the news that Jesus is the way. So let's get out there and do it.

Thank you, Jesus, for dying for our sins to give us a way to the Father. Help us to share that message with others in a way that reflects your love and unconditional forgiveness. We want to point everyone to the way.

Application

1. "Jesus must have been a wonderful person to 'hang out with.' The disciples wanted to be with him." Do you "hang out" with Jesus? Is he as much a part of your everyday life as your closest friends?
2. "We need to give the message, without diminishing the meaning, in a spirit of love. Otherwise it comes across as arrogant and obnoxious." What is your attitude when sharing of Christ being the one and only way to heaven? How can you tell the message of truth in a spirit of love?
3. "We should study all the apologetic material we can get our hands on, because we need to be certain of the truth of Christianity. If we are to say Jesus is the only way, we must be ready to defend the trustworthiness of that statement." Are you completely convinced of the truth of Christianity? How are you prepared to defend the statement that "Jesus is the way"?
4. "People don't reject Christ because they have examined the evidence. They reject him because they really don't want to submit to his authority." Even as a believer, what things do you have trouble submitting to Christ? In what areas is he calling you to complete submission today?
5. "God created you for himself. He created you to know him. You will never be satisfied until you know him." How has knowing God filled the void in your life?

CHAPTER 10

THE TRUTH

JESUS SAID, "I AM THE ROAD, ALSO THE TRUTH, ALSO THE LIFE. NO ONE GETS TO THE FATHER APART FROM ME. IF YOU REALLY KNEW ME, YOU WOULD KNOW MY FATHER AS WELL. FROM NOW ON, YOU DO KNOW HIM. YOU'VE EVEN SEEN HIM!"

PHILIP SAID, "MASTER, SHOW US THE FATHER; THEN WE'LL BE CONTENT."

"YOU'VE BEEN WITH ME ALL THIS TIME, PHILIP, AND YOU STILL DON'T UNDERSTAND? TO SEE ME IS TO SEE THE FATHER. SO HOW CAN YOU ASK, 'WHERE IS THE FATHER?' DON'T YOU BELIEVE THAT I AM IN THE FATHER AND THE FATHER IS IN ME? THE WORDS THAT I SPEAK TO YOU AREN'T MERE WORDS. I DON'T JUST MAKE THEM UP ON MY OWN. THE FATHER WHO RESIDES IN ME CRAFTS EACH WORD INTO A DIVINE ACT."

—JOHN 14:6–10 MSG

A pastor informed his congregation that he would preach a message on honesty and truth the following Sunday. In preparation, he asked them to read the thirty-second chapter of Proverbs during the week.

The next week, prior to his sermon, the pastor said, "Okay, I want to see how many of you did your homework. Raise your hand if you read Proverbs 32 this week."

Hands went up all over the auditorium. Then the pastor explained why he was giving this sermon on honesty and truth: There is no thirty-second chapter in Proverbs!

Truth is an important value that many people lack. It's important to our jobs, to our relationships with our family and friends, and to our relationship with God.

In John 14:6, Jesus claims to be *the* truth. What kind of truth is Jesus talking about? Colossians 1:15 explains that Christ is "the image of the invisible God," the exact likeness of the Father. Jesus is saying, "I'm here to show you the truth about what God is like. I'm going to demonstrate and reveal to you the truth about God."

We grasped in the previous chapter Jesus' claim to be the way to God. He is the only way, the door, the God Gate. Now he says, "Not only am I the way, but I'm also the truth. I will show you what God is all about and what God is like."

Jesus answered Thomas's question about the way, and now he replies to Philip's request in verse 8: "Lord, show us the Father, and that will be enough for us."

> Jesus answered: "Don't you know me, Philip, even after I have been among you such a long time? Anyone who has seen me has seen the Father. How can you say, 'Show us the Father'? Don't you believe that I am in the Father, and that the Father is in me? The words I say to you are not just my own. Rather, it is the Father, living in me, who is doing his work.

Believe me when I say that I am in the Father and the
Father is in me; or at least believe on the evidence of
the miracles themselves." (John 14:9–11)

Jesus basically says to him, "To know the Son is to know the
Father. To see the Son is to see the otherwise invisible God. You
want to see God? Take a look at me."

What does Jesus as the truth reveal in this passage about the
nature of God?

God Is Personal

When the motion picture *Star Wars* was first released, we
began to hear all about "the Force." The Force was everywhere,
surrounding the universe. Many of the basic principles of the
Force can be found in Eastern religions, like the ancient
Chinese philosophy of Taoism.

In the first movie, Obi-Wan Kenobi teaches Luke Skywalker
that he can manipulate the Force if he concentrates hard enough.
Luke attempts to avoid laser blasts from a remote training device
but fails miserably. When Obi-Wan tries it, he has no problems.

In another scene Luke unsuccessfully attempts to lift his
spacecraft out of a swamp. Yoda, a Jedi master who mentors Luke,
effortlessly uses the Force to raise the ship out of the swamp. He
was able to do so because he *believed*, while Luke *doubted*.

Is God like that? Is he some kind of impersonal force out
there around us, in the rocks and in the trees—a force that we
can somehow manipulate?

Through his life in general and this passage in particular,
Jesus demonstrates that God is not an impersonal God. He is
very personal, with a personality, character traits, and attrib-
utes. Most important, God communicates with us.

The Force had no ability to communicate. Rather, people
manipulated it to accomplish good or bad results, depending

on whether they used the good side or the "dark side" of the Force. But Jesus is not a force, and neither is God. He said, "I am the way to God, and I am the truth about God; and just as I am personal, God is personal."

If God is personal and he communicates to us in our lives, I wonder—have I recently gotten to know him a little bit better? In the past few years, have I learned to communicate better with God as he communicates more fully with me? Sometimes we're like Philip. "Lord, if you would just show us God, that would be enough. Lord, if we could just hear the same gentle whisper that Elijah heard there in the cave, that would be sufficient."

Sometimes God seems so remote, so distant, so far away, so impersonal. Have you ever felt that God is remote and impersonal, that you really don't know him? I know I have felt like that at times.

When Philip said, "We want to know God," I'm sure that made Jesus happy. Some people on this planet do not want to know God. There are people who want nothing to do with God. Even if God revealed himself through some kind of miraculous sign, they still wouldn't want to know God. Philip *really* wanted to know God.

But maybe the Lord was also sad because Philip had never made the connection between Jesus and God. Jesus says in verse 9, "Don't you even know who I am? Philip, don't you know who I am after all this time I have been with you?" (author's paraphrase).

Philip had been with Jesus for three years. He'd heard the teaching. He had seen the miracles. He experienced all the things that happened through the Lord during that time, yet he never connected the dots. It's like the person who goes to church all his life and hears about Jesus but never recognizes who Jesus really is and what his responsibility is to Jesus.

Jesus wonders, "Philip, when are you going to get it?" I'm sure he was a little frustrated. "Philip, come on. You've been with me for three years, and you still don't understand." Philip had seen the Lord, but it was the wrong kind of seeing. Have you seen Jesus correctly?

After Jesus' resurrection, when the women reported to the disciples that the tomb was empty, it created quite a stir. Peter and John took off down the road in this footrace to see who could get to the tomb the quickest. John got there first, and he looked in and saw that the tomb was empty.

The Bible uses three different words for the word "see" or "saw" in this passage. The Bible says that John didn't go in, but he looked inside the tomb, and "he *saw* the linen wrappings lying there" (John 20:5 NASB). In other words, his physical eyes were working. The light touched the retina and took the signal to the brain, and John saw that the tomb was empty.

Then, in the next verse, Peter gets to the tomb. He goes inside and *sees* the grave clothes there as well. But he sees that the linens are all folded up. The word "see" is used in a different way. It actually means "to scrutinize, to puzzle over." He is studying everything with his eyes. He is seeing it in a different way.

John finally decides to go into the tomb. The Bible says he "*saw* and believed" (20:8). Here the word means "to perceive" or "to understand."

Philip didn't realize that seeing Jesus meant he had seen the Father—not physically seeing the Father, but truly *seeing (perceiving, understanding)* him. Philip had been with Jesus for three years, but he didn't get it. He didn't really see Jesus. Seeing is not always believing, for Philip saw Jesus, but he didn't really perceive and understand who Jesus was until after the resurrection.

I love the song "Open the Eyes of My Heart." We need to desire to see God, not just physically, but in a way that we perceive and understand who he is. We need to sense his presence. He is a personal God who wants a relationship with you and me. We need to understand who he really is.

Have you perceived him? Have you understood him? Have you come to know him through your experience? If not, why not pray and ask God to open the eyes of your heart and show you the Father.

God Is Love

As we read the Gospels, we see that the love Jesus has for people reveals the nature of God. If you want to know what God is like, look at Jesus.

Jesus lovingly dealt with people. John 13:1 says, "Having loved his own who were in the world, he now showed them the full extent of his love." Why does he love us? I have no idea. It is unexplainable, almost irrational. God certainly does not love us because we are good. The Bible makes that pretty clear. Our lives are full of sin. I can tell you that is true in my own life. God does not love me because I'm such a nice guy or because I'm just a good person. Neither does God love me because I get up on Sunday and open the Bible to teach or preach.

God doesn't need us to do things for him. He doesn't love me because I sing praises to him. He doesn't necessarily need my praise. The Bible says that the heavens are full of beings who praise his name. If we didn't praise him, even the rocks would cry out. He desires and appreciates my praise, but he doesn't need it. He doesn't love me in response to my love for him. I can't say, "Well, God, I love you, so you've got to love me back." The Bible says that he loved us first (1 John 4:19). We would never have loved or even thought of him if he hadn't acted first.

The truth about God is that he is love, and he loves you. That to me is unexplainable. As one Presbyterian minister put it, "The reason God loves is that he loves, and that's it."

There's a great story that's been told for years about Czar Nicholas of Russia. I'm not sure how true it is, but it wonderfully illustrates compassion and forgiveness.

Czar Nicholas placed a young man in charge of an outpost near the border and made him responsible for the pay of his soldiers. The young man did a great job at first. But after awhile, he eventually fell into gambling. In order to get more money, he embezzled the money he was supposed to use to pay the soldiers.

The young man's debt continued to grow until one day he heard an inspector was coming to look at the books. He panicked. He looked to see how much money he owed and what it would cost to pay back what he had taken so nobody would know. He quickly realized he would never be able to repay that debt. He contemplated suicide. He sat staring at the books with revolver in hand. He wrote on a scrap of paper the total amount he owed, and beneath it wrote, "Who can pay so great a debt?"

The man began to get sleepy as he stared at those numbers, and he laid his head down on the desk and fell asleep. While he was sleeping, Czar Nicholas came by. His custom was to dress in peasant clothing and to make his way around to the different outposts to see how things were going. He decided to drop in on the soldier.

Nicholas entered the room and saw the young man sleeping. As he reached down to awaken his friend, he saw the gun and the note. For a moment he thought about arresting his friend, but a wave of compassion came over him. Without waking his friend, he took the little note, wrote one word underneath, and slipped out the door.

Two hours later the man woke up, ready to kill himself. He looked down at that little note, and his eye caught something. On the paper, underneath the words "Who can pay so great a debt?" was the word "Nicholas." He knew immediately that Nicholas had been there. The man realized that if it really was Nicholas, then Nicholas could pay the debt. Two days later, all the money for the debt arrived at the outpost. A few days after that, the inspector came, and everything was fine with the books because Nicholas paid the debt.

God did the same for us to the nth degree. Who could ever pay so great a debt of sin? I can't pay it. I'm not good enough. Who can pay? If we had a little note, there would be one name on it—Jesus. He paid the debt that I owed, and that's why we celebrate Jesus' resurrection from the dead that proves he is God. He paid our debt so we can be clean before the Lord.

Jesus said, "I am the way and the truth," and the truth is that he is the way. Remember when you were young, maybe in middle school, high school, or college, and somebody of the opposite sex liked you? Do you remember what that was like? You sat there and thought to yourself, *Wow, I can't believe that person really likes me.*

Or how about when you stood at your wedding and saw your future spouse at the other end of the aisle. What went through your mind? *I can't believe this person is going to marry me!* We respond in sheer amazement when someone cares for us and wants to be in our presence enough to say, "Yes, I like you. I love you. I want to be with you forever." We should be in that same state of amazement with God.

There have been people who have focused everything on the love of God because they are just enveloped by the thought of God's incredible love. One of them was a young woman named Julian of Norwich. Julian lived in the 1300s. She had a great understanding of God's love. At the age of thirty she received a miraculous healing. From that time on she resided in a little room nestled in the corner of a church building. For the rest of her life she meditated on the love of God.

At one point, Julian wrote, "Some of us believe that God is almighty and may do everything, and that he is all-wisdom and can do everything; but that he is all-love and wishes to do everything—there we stop short. It is this ignorance, it seems to me, that hinders most of God's lovers."[1]

We have somehow missed the point. We don't grasp the incredible love that reaches down to us to sign the note that reads "Who can pay so great a debt?" Jesus is saying, "I can pay it. I'm paying it because I love you so much." That's why Jesus says to Philip, "If you've seen me, you've seen the Father. I am the way to the Father. I am the truth about what God is like."

I mentioned earlier that I have two adult sons. People who have spent time with them often tell me, "Wow, they are just like you!" Whether it's their mannerisms, speech patterns, or the phrases they use, they remind people of me. There is a lot of me in them. We think alike on many things—if you wanted to get to know me and you couldn't be with me, the next best thing would be to talk to my sons.

Just as children reflect their parents in many areas, to an even greater degree Jesus reflects our heavenly Father. That's why Jesus says, "You want to see God? Talk to me. I'll tell you exactly what he's like. I'll show you exactly how he feels. I'll show you exactly how he works because the Father is in me and I am in the Father. I am the truth."

God Is Patient

The third aspect of God that I noticed as I looked at Jesus' conversation with Philip is that he is patient with us. Jesus didn't say, "Philip, you idiot, if you don't get it by now, I'm not going to tell you." That's what we might do. If I had spent three years in almost constant company with someone and that person still didn't understand me, I'd probably say, "Forget it."

But Jesus is patient. He is around these guys who seem to be the epitome of continual failure. Everything they do, they mess up. And Jesus just keeps going after them, teaching them, loving them, and involving them. He never stops. His patience is incredible.

Growing up, I heard so many messages at church about sin and judgment that I began to believe that summarized the message of the Bible. It was important, certainly, because sin is

dangerous. It will destroy your life. But when I attended seminary, I began to realize that the Bible is not predominantly
about sin and judgment. The Bible is predominantly about
God's love, grace, mercy, and patience.

Sin and judgment are subjects the Bible addresses, because it
talks about human sinners. But over and over we see God give
people a chance to live rightly. He loves them through mistake
after mistake after huge sin—and finally, he has to do something. He gave the Israelites hundreds of years to get it right,
because he loved them so much and didn't want them to suffer.

God is patient. As Jesus has his conversation with Philip, he
is not harsh or mean. He lovingly and patiently explains to
Philip, once more, who he is. I can just picture Jesus with his
arm around Philip. "Philip, you've been with me for three years,
pal." Then he explains yet again, "I am the way and the truth
and the life."

Jesus reveals God. "You want to see God?" he asks. "Take a
look at me."

*Heavenly Father, thank you for revealing yourself to us
through your Son. Help us to understand the things he
taught as we learn more about you. Thank you for being
personal, loving, and patient with us and giving us the
ability to have a real, intimate relationship with the God
of the universe.*

Application

1. "Have you ever felt that God is remote and impersonal?" When God feels far away, how do you
   remember that he is a personal God who loves and
   cares about every detail of your life?
2. "Philip had been with Jesus for three years. He'd
   heard the teaching. He had seen the miracles ... yet
   he never connected the dots." What do you know
   about Jesus that you have not yet connected or

applied to your own life? Ask God to open the eyes of your heart to fully "see" this truth.

3. "God doesn't need us to do things for him." What things do you sometimes think you have to do to keep God loving you? How can you trust that he loves you as you are?

4. "We respond in sheer amazement when someone cares for us and wants to be in our presence enough to say, 'Yes, I like you. I love you. I want to be with you forever.' We should be in that same state of amazement with God." How often do you stand in awe of the incredible love God has for you?

5. "Jesus reflects our heavenly Father. That's why Jesus says, 'You want to see God? Talk to me. I'll tell you exactly what he's like.'" What characteristic of God, revealed in Christ Jesus, means the most to you and why? His love, patience, mercy, grace, forgiveness?

CHAPTER 11

THE LIFE

BELIEVE ME: I AM IN MY FATHER AND MY FATHER IS IN ME. IF YOU CAN'T BELIEVE THAT, BELIEVE WHAT YOU SEE—THESE WORKS. THE PERSON WHO TRUSTS ME WILL NOT ONLY DO WHAT I'M DOING BUT EVEN GREATER THINGS, BECAUSE I, ON MY WAY TO THE FATHER, AM GIVING YOU THE SAME WORK TO DO THAT I'VE BEEN DOING. YOU CAN COUNT ON IT. FROM NOW ON, WHATEVER YOU REQUEST ALONG THE LINES OF WHO I AM AND WHAT I AM DOING, I'LL DO IT. THAT'S HOW THE FATHER WILL BE SEEN FOR WHO HE IS IN THE SON. I MEAN IT. WHATEVER YOU REQUEST IN THIS WAY, I'LL DO.

—JOHN 14:11–14 MSG

A parody on the children's book *If You Give a Mouse a Cookie* goes like this:

> If you give a mom a muffin, she will want a cup of coffee to go with it.

She will pour herself some.

Her three-year-old will spill some of the coffee. She'll wipe it up.

Wiping the floor, she'll find dirty socks.

She will remember she has some laundry to do.

When she puts the laundry in the washer, she'll trip over boots and bump into the freezer.

Bumping into the freezer will remind her that she has to plan for supper.

She will get out a pound of hamburger.

She will look for her cookbook, *100 Things to Do with a Pound of Hamburger.*

The cookbook is sitting under a pile of mail.

She will see the phone bill, which is due tomorrow.

She will look for her checkbook.

The checkbook is in her purse that is being dumped out by her two-year-old.

She will smell something funny.

She will change the two-year-old's diaper.

While she is changing the diaper, the phone will ring.

Her five-year-old will answer and hang up.

She will remember she wants to phone a friend for coffee.

Thinking of the coffee will remind her that she was going to have a cup.

She will pour herself some.

And chances are, if she has the cup of coffee, her kids will have eaten the muffin that went with it.

Someone e-mailed that to me one day, and as I read it, I thought, *That's the truth, isn't it?* One thing about moms is they are never bored. There is always something going on. There is always some activity.

Boredom is something we try to avoid. There is something about our nature that avoids boredom. I read the other day about a new roller coaster that is 420 feet high. It goes from zero to 120 miles an hour in four seconds. You go straight up, then start corkscrewing the whole way down. It's two minutes of pure adrenaline!

As I read that, I was thinking of how we always look for ways to get rid of boredom in our lives. Billy Graham once said,

America is said to have the highest per capita boredom of any spot on earth. We know that because we have the greatest number of artificial amusements of any country. People have become so empty that they can't even entertain themselves. They have to pay other people to amuse them, to make them laugh, to try to make them warm and happy and comfortable for a few minutes, to try to lose that awful, frightening, hollow feeling, that terrible dreaded feeling of being lost and alone.[1]

There should never be in the life of any believer an ounce of boredom! Jesus is not only the way and the truth. He is also the life. Many of us look at what is around us and what is going on, and we ask ourselves, "What is life really like? What is it all about?"

Are you excited about life, or are you bored? In verses 12 and 13, Jesus says, "I tell you the truth, anyone who has faith in me will do what I have been doing. He will do even greater things than these, because I am going to the Father. And I will do whatever you ask in my name." That ought to put some spark into your day!

Jesus tells his followers that their lives will never again be the same. He goes on to talk about how the Holy Spirit will come and help them. When the Holy Spirit, the Comforter, comes into your life, your life can never again be drudgery. The life of boredom is impossible.

Jesus told his followers in John 10:10, "I have come that they may have life, and have it to the full." He is talking about your life as a follower of Jesus, as *his* follower. Your life is to be full, a life that is different. He is not referring to eternal life that you must wait for—he is talking about the present life, this life right now.

What is your life like? What is my life like? Does it match up to the kind of life that Jesus said he would give us when we are full of his Spirit? Some Bible translations describe the kind of life he talks about as an "abundant" life. It means "life that was previously unknown."

Jesus says to us, "When you come to me, it doesn't mean all the pain is gone. It doesn't mean all the suffering has been displaced. But it does mean your life will be different, because now I am in you and there is going to be a supernatural side to your life."

Ravi Zacharias said, "Jesus did not come into this world to make bad people good. He came into this world to make dead people live."[2] We should live life to the full!

How many times have you heard kids say, "I'm bored"? If you take a look at their bedroom, you'll notice it's filled with toys, video games, and all kinds of stuff. Yet they still look at you and say, "I'm bored. I need something else." It's incredible.

But as I think about my life, I realize I have said that a few times myself. "I'm bored." Maybe you have, too. But Jesus said the Spirit would indwell us, and from that moment forward our lives would be different. The Comforter gives us a different perspective, a different outlook on life. Jesus says, "I've come to give you a life that is full." If I'm sitting around my house and twiddling my thumbs and say, "I'm bored," a great big alarm should go off in my head. Why am I bored?

Boredom Is Self-Inflicted

Many people feel like they're in a prison of monotony, where every day is the same as the one before. They wake up in the morning and think, *It's just one more day of the same thing. I*

*have to go to the same job. I have to look at the same faces. I have
to deal with the same problems. My life is on a boring track because
I'm always doing the same thing.*

We have believed the lie that tells us life should be one
giant adrenaline rush. So we build the biggest roller coaster, or
we buy the latest gadget or a nicer house. We're always looking for the next thrill that will make our lives a little more
exciting or meaningful. We've all done that. We all yearn for
something that will perk up our lives just a bit and make us
feel a little more at peace and have a teensy bit more meaning
in our lives.

There's a saying I've seen on church bulletin boards: "The
most bored people in life are not the underprivileged, but the
overprivileged." I can certainly attest to that. I've traveled in
many third world countries and seen children playing in the
streets. Sometimes they have a ball and a dirt field; sometimes
they are just playing with rocks and sticks. Most of us would
look at that and ask, "How could they be having fun?"

I've sat in hotels in India where I am surrounded by nothing but poverty. The people are living in huts made out of dirt
and grass, and there is hardly any food. Yet I look out my hotel
window and see kids playing. They're making up games, laugh-
ing, having a great time. They have nothing, but they are able
to make something out of nothing.

For many of us, "fun" requires external stimulation, some
excitement around us, to keep us from getting bored. We get
bored with ourselves. We don't find ourselves very interesting.
All of us have at one time or another bought into the culture's
message that we need to have stuff or life is going to be boring.
Money becomes more important than mothering. Cars become
more important than caring. Houses become more important
than homes. Health becomes more important than healthy
relationships. We have said yes to the wrong things and
inflicted our boredom on ourselves.

Boredom Is Self-Centered

Andrew Murray, another of my favorite authors, wrote, "Self is the root, the branches, the tree, of all the evil of our fallen state."[3] In other words, so many of our problems arise because we look inward and are all about self and selfishness. We don't consider doing for someone else or caring for someone else. We are looking out for our own interests.

That's the beauty of motherhood. Mothers make an incredible sacrifice for their children. They always put the child first. For many of us, however, life has centered around self. And when in our self-centeredness we become bored, we don't blame ourselves. No, we blame it on the other guy. Somebody else is always to blame for our boredom. "That spouse of mine is just not exciting enough."

We expect our bosses, our spouses, and our friends to remove the boredom from our lives. But it doesn't happen, so we get upset. Yet the problem isn't someone else. The problem of boredom is in my life and in my heart.

Boredom Is Self-Pity

What poison is to food, self-pity is to life. Some have called self-pity the most destructive of human emotions. It is destructive because it whines, entangles, and entwines a wide range of harmful emotions like anger, resentment, pride, fear, and bitterness. They are all part of the package deal that self-pity sells us.

Instead of moving on with life, we get stuck. Instead of taking advantage of opportunities, we remain at square one. We stop seeing all that God has for us because our eyes are focused on self. Self-pity shuts out other people and God. It immobilizes us. We look at life and think, *Poor me. Woe is me.* I've had some good pity parties where I just sat there and wallowed in it for a while. But then I realized that something is not quite right. I needed to stop and focus on the ways God has fulfilled his promises in my life.

Boredom Is Self-Perpetuating

One of the great problems with boredom is that we keep making it last longer and longer. Medicine helps us live a little bit longer, but I wonder why certain people want to live longer when they are bored and they're miserable? We want to live long lives, but we often find ourselves with nothing to do on a rainy Sunday afternoon. We go to the doctor's so we can stay healthy and live longer—but then how do we keep entertained?

Relief from boredom will not come from the outside, because it is an issue of the soul. *How, then, does life go from boring to beautiful?*

1. Understand Companionship with Christ

Jesus told Philip that the way to know the Father is to see Jesus. Then he goes further and explains that the Holy Spirit will come to guide us, teach us, give us right thoughts and counsel, and show us how to use our gifts.

Since he couldn't physically be with his disciples forever, Jesus promised to send a Comforter, the Holy Spirit, who would come and indwell them. Instead of having God on the outside, they would have God on the inside. When God comes to dwell in us, how can the world be boring?

Our sinful nature says, "I need this to keep me happy," or "I need this new toy to fill my life." But Jesus says, "That's not what you need. What you need is fellowship with me."

Whenever I get bored and ask myself, "What am I going to do?" there should be a siren that goes off and tells me that maybe I'm looking at the wrong thing. Maybe I'm trying to fill my life with something that I shouldn't be filling it with. Maybe I should just spend some time asking the Lord to fill me with his Spirit. Instead of trying to connect with something external, I need to connect with God, who is in me.

2. Celebrate Life

Another way to keep from being bored is to celebrate life— to sing, to gather together, and to have a good time with feasts and festivals. I really dislike legalism because it takes away the ability to celebrate life. It reduces life to rules and regulations.

As we study Scripture, we see that God constantly encourages his people to celebrate. The Israelites held feasts each year that were both a celebration of what God had done as well as a time to enjoy the blessings of life: harvest, family, music, and good food. They were, for all intents and purposes, parties.

We should also celebrate life, but not just inwardly by counting our blessings. We should do so outwardly and with exuberance. We should celebrate art. We should celebrate music. We should celebrate family and friends. You can celebrate by going to a San Francisco Giants game, but not an A's game (just kidding!). You can celebrate with laughs and by reading your favorite magazine. You can celebrate by spending time with the Lord. We are to enjoy the life God has given us.

I am excited to see a movement in America, as I have visited many churches across the country, that promotes celebration. People are saying, "Okay, my life is hard, and yes, it can be difficult and I am going through some pain right now, but I can still celebrate God's love for me."

The prophet Habakkuk had a great outlook on life. We seem to think we need food, money, status, and security to be happy, and that all those things are what matter in life. Habakkuk wrote,

> Though the fig tree does not bud
>   and there are no grapes on the vines,
> though the olive crop fails
>   and the fields produce no food,

> though there are no sheep in the pen
> and no cattle in the stalls,
> yet I will rejoice in the LORD,
> I will be joyful in God my Savior. (3:17–18)

He said, "Despite the difficulties and disappointments, I will celebrate." Habakkuk knew he could always rejoice in God. Our Savior is watching out for us, teaching us during difficult times, so even then we can celebrate.

Over the years, I hope I have gotten better at celebration, even when things don't line up just the way I want. I'm learning to step back and say, like Habakkuk, "Lord, if everything just falls apart and the house slides off the side of the hill, I can still stop and say, 'You are my God, and I will forever be with you. My soul is safe, and I'll be with you forever and ever. I will celebrate your presence in my life.'"

Why is it important? When I look out my kitchen window and I watch the sunset, I need to celebrate the sunset. I need to revel in the sunset. I need to enjoy the color. I need to enjoy the movement of the sun. I need to celebrate that sunset because when I do, I'm celebrating the One who made the sunset. I'm looking at the creation of God and saying, "God, I love it. It's all around me, and because of that I want to celebrate you and I want to thank you for what you've given me in this world." That's what makes life beautiful and worth living.

3. Cultivate New Life in Others

Another pursuit that makes life more beautiful is to cultivate new life in others. Jesus told his disciples, "When the Spirit comes and indwells you, you're going to do the things I have been doing—and you're going to do even greater things than I have done."

Scholars and theologians have pondered this one for years. What did Jesus actually mean? That's a pretty heavy statement.

Most scholars agree that this passage refers to people coming to the Lord. "You will do greater things," he said. How could he say that?

If you look at the life of Jesus during the three and a half years of his ministry on earth, he left about five hundred followers when he ascended back into heaven. But Jesus said, "Stick around, because while you're gathered here the Holy Spirit is going to come upon you."

We read in the book of Acts how the Holy Spirit came and the disciples held the first-ever evangelistic crusade. On one occasion, three thousand people came to the Lord! Three thousand more people were now followers of Jesus. That's why Jesus said to them, "You're going to do greater things than I am doing." Jesus only preached in Palestine. He didn't move out from that area. When the Spirit came upon his disciples, they fanned out across the world. They went to faraway places where thousands heard the gospel. And since that time, many more millions have believed in Jesus.

A man recently told me how his son had led someone to the Lord, and he was so excited. One of the greatest joys in the world is to talk to someone about the Lord. Want your life to be more exciting? Find someone to witness to. Even if they reject you, it's exciting. When we start looking for someone else to connect with and share the greatest news ever with, that's exciting!

You can start out slowly. Find a common interest or hobby. Build a bridge, a relationship that will allow them to get a chance to trust you. If you're in a situation where your life is boring, stop and say, "Okay, forget all the stuff and material things that I look for to satisfy me from the outside. What's happening in my life on the inside?"

What have we tried to hold on to that we thought would be the answer to the boredom in our lives? Is it that new car? Is it a new house?

All these things are enjoyable, but God never meant for them to satisfy our souls. They were never meant to take away the boredom of life. They are amenities we can enjoy, but they become unenjoyable when we do not know the Lord. How many bored people live in big houses and drive fancy cars but are still absolutely bored with life? Jesus says, "I have come to give life and to give it to the full right now." Not just in eternity, but right now.

The next time you find yourself bored with life, ask yourself, "Am I looking to the wrong things for fulfillment? Am I looking in the wrong places?"

If that describes your life, confess it to God as sin. Tell him, "Lord, I'm sorry. I've been looking in the wrong spot, and I want to look to you. You are my source of life."

God, I take complete responsibility for my own boredom. My life is supernaturally filled by your Holy Spirit, and if I am bored, that means I have allowed something else in my life that probably should not be there. I am worshipping something else. Help me to lift my hands and my heart to you alone, Lord.

Application

1. As Jesus' follower, yours should be a life that is full, a life that is different. How does following Jesus make your life full and different from those around you?
2. "All of us have at one time or another bought into the culture's message that we need to have stuff or life is going to be boring. We have said yes to the wrong things and inflicted our boredom on ourselves." How have you inflicted boredom on yourself? What worthless things have you pursued, and what worthwhile and fulfilling pursuits have you neglected?

3. "So many of our problems arise because we look inward and are all about self and selfishness. We are looking out for our own interests." What opportunities do you have to find joy and fulfillment by looking outward and helping to meet the needs of others?

4. "Our Savior is watching out for us, teaching us during difficult times, so even then we can celebrate." What can you celebrate about your life today, even in difficult times?

5. "One of the greatest joys in the world is to talk to someone about the Lord. Want your life to be more exciting? Find someone to witness to." Who can you begin to build a relationship with in order to share the message of salvation?

JESUS, OUR VINE

CHAPTER 12

THE TRUE VINE

I AM THE REAL VINE AND MY FATHER IS THE FARMER.
HE CUTS OFF EVERY BRANCH OF ME THAT DOESN'T BEAR
GRAPES. AND EVERY BRANCH THAT IS GRAPE-BEARING
HE PRUNES BACK SO IT WILL BEAR EVEN MORE. YOU ARE
ALREADY PRUNED BACK BY THE MESSAGE I HAVE SPOKEN.

—JOHN 15:1–3 MSG

One Sunday I drove home from a speaking engagement along California's coastal highway. As we headed out of Los Angeles, we began to see vineyards popping up all over the place. In fact, the area from Santa Barbara to Morgan Hill, about a 250-mile stretch, seemed to have grown into one big vineyard.

We just gazed in amazement out our windows as we wound through the beautiful countryside. One vineyard after another made it look like a sea of grapes—it was absolutely beautiful.

Jesus uses the analogy of a vineyard to describe his relationship with us. He says in John 15:5, "I am the vine; you are the branches. If a man remains in me and I in him, he will bear much fruit; apart from me you can do nothing." He calls the Father (v. 1) the gardener, or vinedresser. Everyone has a role in God's vineyard.

The Vine

When I first came to the Lord, I had a hard time visualizing this passage. I didn't grow up around vineyards. I've always had a hard time picturing Jesus as the Vine and us as branches because in my mind the vine is smaller than the branches.

I grew up in Bishop Estates, California. We had two walnut trees in our backyard, and they made a huge mess each year as the walnuts dropped to the ground and rotted. But because of those walnut trees, when I sometimes read John 15, I would substitute some words in my head. Instead of the vine and the branches, I would picture Jesus as the trunk and us as the branches. With that picture in my head, I had a little better understanding of what he was asking of me. But as I grew older, I came to appreciate how powerful the analogy of the vine is.

Jesus called himself the "true vine" (v. 1). He was genuine, real, authentic. Whenever Jesus used an illustration, he would pick something that made sense to his audience. We have to take ourselves back to that context to best understand his point. Since Israel was full of vineyards, his listeners understood what he meant.

Jesus and his disciples were probably walking by a vineyard when Jesus gave them this message. The Israelites were very familiar with vineyards. The temple even had a "golden vine" above it to remind the people that God in the Old Testament saw Israel as his "vine" or "vineyard."

Isaiah 5 provides a beautiful description of God's concern for his vineyard, the children of Israel. Hosea 10:1 says, "Israel was a spreading vine; he brought forth fruit for himself." So

when Jesus says, "I am the true vine," his Jewish listeners identified with that image.

Unfortunately, however, many of the passages where God
describes Israel as a vine refer to their rebellion and wandering.
Jeremiah 2:21 says, "I had planted you like a choice vine of
sound and reliable stock. How then did you turn against me into
a corrupt, wild vine?" In Isaiah 5:4 God laments, "What more
could have been done for my vineyard than I have done for it?
When I looked for good grapes, why did it yield only bad?"

God wanted them to produce sweet fruit, but they brought
forth only sour grapes. They followed after foreign gods and
idols, and their hearts were full of rebellion. God wanted to
bless them. He wanted to see them bear the choicest fruit, but
their hearts were far from him.

The picture of Israel as the vine that the Old Testament provides isn't pretty. They consistently wander and rebel. They just
tell God, "In your face. I'm out of here. I'm going in a different
direction." Yet God's heart pursues them. He mourns for them.
God gives them that free choice, the wonderful gift he continues to extend to us today. Israel had a choice. They could follow
after God and be part of his vineyard, or they could turn the
other way and do whatever they wanted.

People have asked, "Did God create evil?" God did not create evil, but he allowed for the possibility of evil. He gave us a
choice. We can choose to follow God, or we can choose to go in
a different direction. God could get rid of evil on the earth, but
then he would also have to get rid of love, because they are both
choices. We can choose evil, or we can choose to love God. He
doesn't force us to make either choice. Although he may discipline us and point out our need to mend our ways, God gives us
the final choice of whether or not we want to follow him.

Jesus says, "I am the true vine; all others are substitutes.
All the other vines have no power to satisfy your soul. They
will not bring you joy and life, and you will only experience

emptiness. But I am the true vine. Be connected with me. Be grafted into me."

I don't know where you are. We all go through times when, just like Israel, we are far from God. We are producing sour grapes. We have all done and said things we knew we shouldn't. We've chosen to head in a different direction. God says to us, "Listen, it is your choice, but I would prefer if you would come back to me." What a horrible thing it would be for the Lord to say of us that we are a wild vine producing sour grapes. He wants to bless us but waits for us to make the right choice.

The Branches

There are two kinds of branches. There are healthy branches and unhealthy branches, those that bear fruit and those that do not. Some branches are alive, green, and fruitful; others are barren, brown, and dead. They are brittle and fruitless.

I don't know what kind of branch you are right now. But this passage of Scripture causes me to pause and evaluate my spiritual growth. Jesus said, "I am the vine; you are the branches." What do our branches look like? Are they producing fruit?

There are unhealthy branches in every vineyard. The farmer doesn't leave those branches there very long. He must remove them in order to prevent the spread of disease, molds, and blight that can spread to the healthy branches.

There are unhealthy branches in the church as well. Leading church analysts like George Barna have reported that more than 80 percent of churches in America are either in a plateau or declining in their numbers. The average size of a church in America is just over one hundred people in attendance. But the most amazing statistic is that the average minister now stays in one church for only five years, and the average time in ministry is seventeen years.

When I think of that in light of the church in America, I realize there must be some unhealthy branches out there. These churches are not producing fruit. If we produce fruit, then over time, our numbers will expand—not for the sake of numbers, but for the sake of the fruit. A healthy branch will produce fruit; an unhealthy branch doesn't produce anything good.

There are people who are mechanically attached to Christ like a branch that is grafted into a vine, but it doesn't really "take." There are those who believe the truths of Christianity and are visible members of a church but lack a living faith in Christ. Their souls are not open to spiritual transformation. There is no fruit. Their Christian life is merely a charade, and they have utterly quenched and grieved the Holy Spirit. They operate under the influence of their flesh, and they don't even know it.

We've all experienced similar times when we've thought, *Oh, everything is great.* But we're often just living off past experiences or relying on some verse we memorized years and years ago. There is no life. There is no fruit. There is no change of character, change of personality, change of habits. Nothing has changed. To God, that's a dead branch.

One of the most important aspects of bearing fruit is in our character. In Mark 4, verses 18 and 19, Jesus speaks about different types of soil and says, "Still others, like seed sown among thorns, hear the word; but the worries of this life, the deceitfulness of wealth and the desires for other things come in and choke the word, making it unfruitful."

In the Lord's mind, the fact that we go to church on Sunday morning is not the issue. The question to the Lord is, Are we bearing fruit in our lives? Can we see evidence of the Holy Spirit living in us and operating through us? Just because a church has lots of branches doesn't make it a healthy church. The key question is, "Do you see any fruit?"

You may attend a huge church, but size may not be an indicator of health. Many of the people who attend megachurches did not come as new believers to Christ there. They came from other churches. Just because a church has thousands of members, it is not necessarily a sign of health. A healthy church, according to Jesus, is one that bears fruit. Are they bearing fruit in terms of souls won to Christ? Christlike character? Love?

Let's thank God, though, for the healthy branches. They enjoy a true connection to the Vine. Spiritual life flows from Christ through his Holy Spirit to those healthy branches. That is what "spiritual formation" is all about.

Spiritual formation is a new phrase for something that may already be familiar to you. The old term is what we call "discipleship." For years, we've used the word *discipleship* to refer to growth in character and Christlikeness. Discipleship and spiritual formation are really the same thing. It is basically the changing of our character to become more like the character of Christ. It is the ongoing surrender of our intellect, will, and emotions to the influence of the Spirit of God. That is the healthy branch. The healthy branch is one that bears fruit, the one that is being changed, the one that experiences ongoing transformation.

I once spoke with a pastor who was discouraged with the youth ministry at his church. They had lots of kids in it, and to get all the way through the program, the teens would memorize hundreds of verses. But the pastor was frustrated because he wasn't seeing fruit. He said, "These young people who go through this program have memorized around seven hundred verses. But it seems to have little lasting impact on their lives after they graduate."

After our conversation, I began to wonder if memorizing verses for the sake of getting a piece of candy or promotion to the next rank in the organizational structure is the best motivation for Scripture memorization. I am supposed to memorize Bible verses so I can become more like Christ, right? If I'm just memorizing verses for the sake of memorizing them or to brag about how much I know, what good is it? If I don't take it in and intend to live what I have memorized, what have I really accomplished? I'm like the person described in James 1:23–24 who looks in the mirror, then walks away and forgets what he looks like.

Healthy branches experience the life of the Spirit flowing through them. Healthy branches have a common interest in Jesus, common desires, and a common destiny. Healthy branches enjoy a union of friendship, love, dependence, obedience, and submission to Christ. That's a healthy branch.

Jesus is the Vine, and we are the branches. There are going to be healthy branches and unhealthy branches. Our responsibility is to do everything we can to be healthy specimens. If we're unhealthy, we need to take steps to move toward health. We need to get some help along the way.

The Gardener

The key player who helps us along the way is God himself. He is the farmer, the gardener, the vinedresser, the sole proprietor and owner of the vineyard. He answers to no one. He alone cares for the vineyard, for the vines; and he alone knows what he is doing. He tends the vineyard, waters it, cultivates it, and makes it produce the maximum amount of fruit possible. That is what we discover as we read further through this passage in John 15.

This farmer or gardener fills a number of roles. Verse 2 says, "He cuts off every branch in me that bears no fruit, while every branch that does bear fruit he prunes so that it will be even more fruitful." Then in verse 6 he says, "If anyone does not remain in me, he is like a branch that is thrown away and withers; such branches are picked up, thrown into the fire and burned."

These verses are a little frightening. We are more comfortable with the passages about love. But Jesus clearly states that the unhealthy branches will be "cut off." What does that mean?

Some interpret it to mean God may take somebody home to heaven prematurely, especially if that person is destroying his testimony (see Acts 5:1–11; 1 Cor. 11:30). But is that what he is talking about in this passage?

I'm not a proprietor of a vineyard, but I did go to Ask.com, and I asked, "How do I grow grapes?" The search results directed me to sites that told me how to grow a vineyard. Articles explained that the branches grow and then droop onto the ground. If the branches rest on the ground, you're not going to have any grapes. They can't get enough sunlight or water in that position, and the air can't circulate properly among the branches.

The farmer comes along and takes the branches off the ground and weaves them around the wire, and that's how you start having a healthy vineyard. The word that is translated "cuts off" can also be translated "lifts up." It makes sense when you read about how a vineyard is actually grown.

I believe that the Father, the farmer, "lifts us up" when we're not growing properly. Yes, there may come a time when he cuts us off, but not before he lifts us up.

Remember when you first came to the Lord? In that early time of learning how to walk with him, did the Lord lift you up and draw you into true devotion to him? Even in the midst of your failures, you knew he was there to lift you up and to encourage your heart. It is such a wonderful thing to be lifted up. Jesus is saying, "That's what the Father does. If you're a real branch, if you've got a little bit of life left in you at all, he is going to come along and lift you up and put you back on that wire and weave you around securely so you can produce more fruit."

I heard a story about the captain of a battleship who was trying to steer his vessel through some dense fog at night back in the 1950s. He saw some lights directly in front of him, so he sent a signal to the other ship, saying, "Alter your course ten degrees south."

The captain immediately received a response, "No, you alter your course ten degrees south."

That made the captain pretty upset, so he signaled, "I am a captain of the U.S. Navy. I strongly suggest you alter your course ten degrees south. I am a battleship."

The reply came back immediately. "I am a lighthouse. I suggest you alter your course ten degrees south."

We sometimes do that. We're in the dark, and we think we have it all figured out. But the Lord says to us, "No, you alter your course. I am the farmer. I'm going to lift you up. I'm going to encourage your heart. I'm going to bless you. I'm going to move in your life. I'm going to teach you. I'm going to help you to produce the maximum amount of fruit that you can produce in your life. Therefore, I am asking you to alter your course." God continually asks us to adjust to his will and to his ways.

Another word that Jesus uses in verse 2 is "prune" or "trim." Another lesson I learned from my research was that grapes will only grow on new branches. They don't grow on old branches. The farmer trims back those branches. Prune to the right length, so that next year a new growth appears, and that's where the grapes come from. But you're never going to grow healthy and abundant grapes on an old branch. The farmer continually prunes the branches each year to prepare them for the new crop. It's a process of pruning, growing, fruit bearing, and pruning once again. If that process ever stops, there can be no harvest. There will be no fruit.

As we examine our lives, we need to ask ourselves, "Have I matured in my Christian life? Has the Lord pruned me to the point that I am maturing and bearing fruit?"

I confess there are days I don't want to be mature. There are days I don't want to forgive. There are days I don't want to be compassionate. There are days when I don't want to go the extra mile. I don't want to listen. I don't want to follow God's priorities. I have days like that.

But there are other days, wonderful days, when I see that glimmer of growth in my life. It brings me joy and hope. I can say with delight, "Wow, Lord, I'm growing."

I recently underwent a test of my maturity. I had composed a rather scathing e-mail to someone. It was there on the screen, ready to send, and it was a *clever* one. It was going to set that person straight. But as my hand wandered over to click on Send, I thought about what I was doing, and I hit Delete instead. The computer prompted me, "Are you sure you want to delete this message?" I punched Y on the keyboard. I then walked away from the computer. As I got up from my desk, I thought, *Thank you, Lord. I'm certainly not perfect. I mess up all the time. I am a very impatient individual. But, Lord, for this day, for this moment, for right now, this was such a wonderful victory just to delete it and walk away from it.*

Ask yourself if you have matured over the last few years. God wants his vineyard to mature. He wants to see new growth. Do the people who know you—those who live, work, and spend time with you—see a difference in your life?

How do you know you're a live branch? How do you know you're filled with the Spirit of God? Are you producing fruit? If there is no fruit, you are a dead branch. If there is no fruit, the Lord says, "I've got to do something here because the deadness of that branch is going to impact the rest of the vineyard." That's God's pruning.

Sometimes I wonder if I can resist God's pruning. He at times lets me grow my own way. But the times in my life when I've tried to grow in a million different directions, any way but the way that God wants, are the times when I have produced no fruit.

I don't like the thought of being cut off. The thought of that doesn't sit well with me. But the notion of him lifting me up brings great hope and comfort. The Lord knows my struggles, and he knows your struggles, your weaknesses. When we're down, the Lord comes to us through his Spirit, lifts us up, and says, "I'm going to put you back on that vine. I'm going to put you back on that wire because I want you to produce, I want you to grow, and I want fruit to come from your life."

Only you and the Lord know where you are. Be honest with yourself. Don't play games and deceive yourself into thinking you can simply go through the motions of being a Christian. There needs to be real fruit, the fruit of the Spirit—love, joy, peace, patience, kindness, goodness, faithfulness, gentleness, and self-control. There needs to be the fruit of character, the fruit of being a witness for him.

If not, then we are dead branches. There is no way around it. We can't conclude anything else. We're dead, and we need his help, and we need that sap to flow back through us to produce life once again.

Father, make us open to your pruning in our lives. Help us desire to grow your way, to be fruitful, to be part of a healthy vineyard. Thank you for Jesus, our Vine, who nourishes us and gives us the strength to be vibrant, growing believers.

Application

1. "God wanted to bless them. He wanted to see them bear the choicest fruit, but their hearts were far from him." Are you missing out on God's blessings by turning your heart from him? What choice fruit is he calling you to bear instead?
2. "One of the most important aspects of bearing fruit is in our character." Does your character bear the fruit of living in the Vine? Are you daily becoming more like Christ?
3. "If I don't take it in and intend to live Bible verses I have memorized, what have I really accomplished?" What do you do with the Bible verses you learn? Do

you allow them to impact the way you live?

4. "God continually asks us to adjust to his will and to his ways." How is God asking you to adjust to his will in order to help you become more fruitful?

5. "There are other days, wonderful days, when I see that glimmer of growth in my life. It brings me joy and hope." What glimmers of growth have you recently seen in your life? How does that encourage you to continue to strive toward maturity in Christ?

CHAPTER 13

REMAIN IN ME

LIVE IN ME. MAKE YOUR HOME IN ME JUST AS I DO IN YOU. IN THE SAME WAY THAT A BRANCH CAN'T BEAR GRAPES BY ITSELF BUT ONLY BY BEING JOINED TO THE VINE, YOU CAN'T BEAR FRUIT UNLESS YOU ARE JOINED WITH ME.

I AM THE VINE, YOU ARE THE BRANCHES. WHEN YOU'RE JOINED WITH ME AND I WITH YOU, THE RELATION INTIMATE AND ORGANIC, THE HARVEST IS SURE TO BE ABUNDANT. SEPARATED, YOU CAN'T PRODUCE A THING. ANYONE WHO SEPARATES FROM ME IS DEADWOOD, GATHERED UP AND THROWN ON THE BONFIRE.

—JOHN 15:4–6 MSG

When I was five years old, my family bought our first color television. I remember the first time my father turned it on, and I suddenly saw everything in color.

The first image I saw was the old NBC peacock. I watched in amazement as it spread its feathers just before a show. Then *Bonanza* came on, right there, in living color.

I had watched black-and-white television for years, and now it was in brilliant color—radiant and alive.

Jesus says to us, "When you are connected to me, you will truly be alive." Verse 4 reads, "Remain in me, and I will remain in you. No branch can bear fruit by itself; it must remain in the vine. Neither can you bear fruit unless you remain in me."

The King James Version uses the word "abide," and the New International Version translates it "remain." So what does this word really mean? What does it mean to abide, to remain in Christ?

We are the branches, and we are connected to the Vine—Jesus Christ—through whom life flows. This should not be something abnormal or unusual in our experience. Rather, it should be the norm. If you remain and abide in him, there will take place a spiritual awakening.

The Gospels repeatedly portray how people who come into vital contact with Jesus can't go away unchanged. Their lives go from empty and dull to full and exciting. When we say yes to Jesus, we truly begin to live. Jesus came to turn black-and-white living into living color.

Andrew Murray wrote a little book called *Abide in Christ*. He wrote in the preface,

> It is to be feared that there are many earnest followers of Jesus from whom the meaning of this word [abide], with the blessed experiences it promises, is very much hidden. While trusting in their Savior for pardon and for help, and seeking to some extent to obey Him, they have hardly realized to what closeness of union, to what intimacy of fellowship, to what wondrous oneness of life and interest, He invited them when He said,

"Abide in me." This is not only an unspeakable loss to themselves, but the church and the world suffer in what they lose.[1]

Many people regard salvation as a onetime event that takes place, and then we just walk away, saying, "Okay, I took care of that. Now I can live any way I want." They "prayed the prayer," and they're going to heaven, so there's no point in doing anything else.

Murray points out in his book that there is an old phrase called "union and communion." When we open our hearts to Jesus, it is the beginning of union and communion with Christ. Yes, we accept him into our life, but we can't just walk away and say, "Okay, I did that," or "Heaven is my home, and everything is wonderful."

No, it begins this new relationship. Jesus said, "You are the branches. I am the Vine. You have to stay connected to me. I am the source of life and joy. All fruit, joy, satisfaction, and life come from your commitment to abide with me."

That's why this thing we call the Christian life needs to match up with the expectations of the Bible. God has high expectations of his people. When Jesus came, he raised those expectations even higher. Jesus told us we would bear fruit. If you are truly one of his, you will bear fruit. Fruit bearing is not to be the exception. It is the standard.

Have you asked yourself: How do I remain with Jesus? We pray, read the Bible, and sing worship songs to him. But how do we *remain* with him? Jesus says in the passage, "Remain in me, and I will remain in you." There is a part that we each have to do to remain in him.

When I was a young man and first started attending church, Pentecost Sunday wasn't talked about a lot. But Pentecost Sunday in the early church was a time of celebration. It was the church's birthday.

Acts 2 tells the story of the miraculous events that surrounded this day,

> When the day of Pentecost came, they were all
> together in one place. Suddenly a sound like the
> blowing of a violent wind came from heaven and
> filled the whole house where they were sitting. They
> saw what seemed to be tongues of fire that separated
> and came to rest on each of them. All of them were
> filled with the Holy Spirit and began to speak in other
> tongues as the Spirit enabled them. (vv. 1–4)

From that point on, the church began to grow. The apostles
preached, and three thousand people were saved in one day (v.
41). There was a new union—a new unity. There was a new power
as the church was born. A new revolution had begun.

In my early days as a Christian I heard a lot about Christmas
and Easter and other special days and very little about Pentecost
Sunday. But this abiding in Christ cannot happen without the
Holy Spirit! It is impossible. Without the Spirit, without the flow
of the Spirit into your life, there can be no abiding. We may fool
ourselves into thinking we're abiding, but unless the Spirit is alive
in you and controlling your life, you are not really abiding.

When my wife and I were first married, we took a vacation
down to San Diego, the location of my favorite Christian bookstore in the world—the Evangelical Bookstore. It is enormous.
One of the books I bought there was by R. A. Torrey, entitled
The Holy Spirit: Who He Is and What He Does. I hadn't heard
much about the Holy Spirit. I went to college and took Bible
courses, but I wasn't quite satisfied with my education in that
area. So I picked up this book, and that weekend I read through
the whole thing.

I already knew that Torrey was an evangelist, a pastor, an
educator, and a brilliant scholar. He served as pastor of Moody
Church in Chicago. While he was pastor there, his church

would allow him to go away for several months at a time to do evangelistic work overseas. He was also the dean and president of what we now know as Biola University. Torrey was also instrumental in the growth of Moody Bible Institute in Chicago. He was a man who was not afraid of the Holy Spirit. He knew the importance of the Holy Spirit, and he refused to let the Holy Spirit become a second-class citizen in the church that the Holy Spirit had empowered.

As he spoke, Torrey would continually preach the ministry of the Holy Spirit. Back in those days Christians used phrases like "baptized in the Spirit" and the "anointing of the Holy Spirit." When people say to me, "I'm going to pray that the Lord anoints you for this occasion," I am encouraged, because I really believe in the Holy Spirit's work.

But the primary reason I picked up Torrey's book was my dissatisfaction with my own Christian experience. My second reason was that I wanted to make sure that when I was in ministry and doing the Lord's work, the Holy Spirit's power would flow through me to accomplish the purpose for which God had called me.

I picked up another book, this one by A. W. Tozer—a fascinating man—a great writer and thinker. He wrote a tiny book called *How to Be Filled with the Holy Spirit*.

I was twenty-three years old and a youth pastor at Fair Oaks Baptist Church when I read those two books by those two great men of God. They helped me to understand the Holy Spirit.

Who Is the Holy Spirit?

The Holy Spirit is the Spirit of God. He is everywhere and penetrates everything. No physical matter can stop the Spirit. He permeates your body. He sees into your mind. He surrounds you when you are at work. He rides with you in your car. The Holy Spirit of God goes anywhere he wants.

The Holy Spirit is not an "it," a force, or an enthusiastic feeling. The Holy Spirit is a person who possesses a will, intelligence, and emotions. He can hear and see. He can express himself in language. The Holy Spirit of God has personality.

Some people incorrectly think of the Holy Spirit as an "it," some supernatural force that is similar to "the Force" in the *Star Wars* movies. But the Holy Spirit is a person. He is the third person of the Trinity.

Tozer was dismayed by the lack of the Spirit's fullness in his people. They believed in the Spirit, but nobody seemed to be experiencing him. Something was wrong. As Tozer looked at his congregation, he saw they were committed to fundamentalism, but it was powerless. There seemed to be nothing happening; the Holy Spirit was not active. For us to be connected to the Vine and have the spiritual sap flowing through us, we must be filled with the Holy Spirit.

So how does that happen? The Bible teaches us that when we open our heart to Jesus, at that moment the Spirit of God comes in. We've already looked at John chapter 3, where Jesus tells Nicodemus, "You have to be born of water, physical birth— but you also have to be born of the Spirit."

The moment we say, "Jesus, come into my life," the Spirit of God comes and fills us. That is the beginning of the renovation of the heart. It's what we call regeneration. Two natures then begin their struggle for control in our life. There's the old, sinful nature, which is definitely still there; and there is the new nature, which is the product of the Spirit of God who indwells us.

Dr. Kenneth Wuest, a professor of Greek who taught at Moody Bible Institute for years, said this about the Holy Spirit: "It is not putting gas in the tank but a driver at the wheel."[2]

We often think of the Holy Spirit as gas in our tank. We say, "Fill me up and now away we go. I'll stay behind the wheel, though, if you don't mind." We think we only need to get our tank filled up once a week in church, and then it will be smooth sailing. But it's not just about filling your tank. It's about putting him in the driver's seat. It's saying, "Okay, Lord, you can drive."

We want to drive our own lives. I know I do. We say to God, "I'm not going to do that," or "I don't want to go there," and we take back the steering wheel. We push God out of the driver's seat and relegate the Holy Spirit to the role of backseat driver. That's a place he doesn't want to be.

The Spirit can indwell us without controlling us. Yes, when you open your heart to Christ and say, "Jesus, come into my life," the Spirit of God invades your life. But it doesn't mean that the Holy Spirit of God has control of your life today. We have the ability to take back control. We can for a while get along without him. We can live life our own way. After all, who wants to yield to someone else? Who wants to be in submission to the Holy Spirit? But if we do not give up that control, we can't be filled with the Spirit. We will be running life in the power of our own flesh.

God does not want you simply to be religious, going through the motions every week in church. He wants to invade every area of your life through the Holy Spirit. Ephesians 5:18 says, "Do not get drunk on wine, which leads to debauchery. Instead, be filled with the Spirit." Be filled with the Holy Spirit. The question is: Do we really *want* the Holy Spirit to control us?

No matter where you come from, or whatever your theological understanding of the Holy Spirit may be, the question remains: Do we really want to be controlled by the Holy Spirit? Are we truly willing to have God live his life through us? Do we really want to give up the reins? Do we really want to submit? Do we really want to be obedient?

The verb "to fill" also means "to control." To be *filled* with the Spirit means to be *controlled* by the Holy Spirit. Is that what we really want? Are we sure we want the personality of God to permeate our hearts and minds, directing us to do what he wants?

To be filled with the Spirit is an ongoing experience. It's not a onetime event. We also have the ability to quench and grieve the Spirit of God. Paul wrote in Ephesians 4:30, "And do not grieve the Holy Spirit of God, with whom you were sealed for the day of redemption." Then in 1 Thessalonians 5:19, he said, "Do not quench the Spirit" (NASB).

We can offend the Holy Spirit, and then we need to confess our sin, saying, "Lord, forgive me. I want to be controlled by your Spirit." It's something we continually need to do.

Ephesians 5:18 is not a suggestion. "Well, if you *want* to be filled and under control of the Spirit, go ahead." No, it's a command: "Be filled with the Spirit." It's not an option.

I was rummaging through some of my stuff the other day, and I came across something I had nearly forgotten about. It was from my journal.

> At one Jesus Festival two years ago $98,000 worth of Jesus paraphernalia was sold: clocks, watches, wallets, mugs, etc. Today you see more cars driving around with fish decals or a beautiful rainbow with the words "Born Again" underneath it. There are more religious TV shows than ever before. You can listen to Christian radio twenty-four hours a day, offering material and everything from Bible exposition to how to handle your finances. The Christian bookstore has grown in popularity. There you can get a book on any problem you might have. You can buy Christian rock records so you can show your young people that Christianity is keeping up with the times. Now there are even Christian videos and movies you can show at home to replace the trash that is on television.
>
> We have Christian counselors and psychologists, Christian attorneys, Christian doctors,

Christian bankers and, yes, even Christian mechan-
ics. But have you noticed with all these fifty million
born-again Christians and all the helps and advice
we have, Christianity is still losing ground? Sin continues to increase, crime rate goes up. Alcoholism
goes up. Prostitution goes up. Morality is still slip-
ping away, and here in the local church a large
percent of the Christians are defeated, depressed,
discouraged, and despondent. Are we happy, satisfied, fulfilled, and living in victory over sin? Most
are not.

What's the problem? Our problem is our lack of
understanding as to the Holy Spirit, who he is and
what he does. Sermons are preached on God. The
Christian is to walk with God; that's his purpose.
Sermons are preached on Christ. The Christian is to
walk after Christ; that's his pattern. Sermons
should be preached on the Holy Spirit. The
Christian is to walk in the Spirit. Why? Because
that's his power. It seems as if the charismatics have
so overemphasized the Holy Spirit and have created
an imbalance in their teachings that we have over-
reacted by not talking about the Holy Spirit at all.
We are unbalanced. The people and the church
without the Holy Spirit have no power. We need to
be filled with the Spirit.

—DAN OWENS
FAIR OAKS BAPTIST CHURCH, 1981

I wrote that journal entry during the time I was reading the
books by Torrey and Tozer. I had come to a profound realization. "Lord, I accepted you as my Savior, you filled me with
your Spirit, but since that time I have not been taught."

How Can We Be Filled with the Spirit?

There are four steps I need to follow in order to be continually filled with the Spirit. They are actually quite simple.

The first is *confess sin*. First John 1:9 says, "If we confess our sins, he is faithful and just and will forgive us our sins and purify us from all unrighteousness." We can quench the Spirit by a failure to respond to his promptings and leadings. We can grieve the Spirit by involvement in sinful behavior that we are aware is wrong. We need to confess daily, "Spirit of God, please forgive me."

The second step is *submit to God*. We need to say, "Lord, I choose to submit myself to the control of the Spirit of God. I want the Spirit of God to control me."

Third, *ask the Lord to fill you*. Pray that God will fill you and control you by the Spirit.

Finally, *thank him for that filling*. By faith give thanks to him, saying, "Thank you, Father, for filling me with your Holy Spirit."

Back in those early days of my Christian walk and ministry, I really wasn't taught that process. I had never learned about the ministry of the Holy Spirit in the life of the believer. We need to be connected to Jesus, our Vine. We also need his life-giving spiritual sap to flow through us. We need to be filled with the Spirit of God.

We grow a lot of plants in our backyard. Whenever my wife picks flowers from our yard, they become disconnected from the live-giving source of the vine or stem to which they were attached. It isn't long before they wither and die. Even though for a while they will look like they're alive, in just a few days they will be quite obviously dead.

We disrupt our connection with the Vine and his life-giving power by the sin we tolerate in our lives. We disconnect ourselves through disobedience. We disconnect by saying, "Oh Lord, I don't want you." For a while we may continue to appear healthy. We may even continue to read our Bibles, to go to church, and to participate in Christian activities. But our disconnected state results in a loss of fellowship with God, which eventually makes itself known in a withered and dead spirituality. Even though we are saved, our relationship with our Father is nearly nonexistent.

As you go through your week and you realize there is something wrong in your life, I encourage you to pray, "Lord, forgive me. Lord, I want to submit myself to you. Spirit of God, I want you to control me. I want you to fill me with your presence. I want you to take over my thoughts, and I want you to take over my life, and I want to thank you for that filling."

Jesus said, "Remain in me, and I'll remain in you." What's our responsibility? Our responsibility is to keep a "short sin account." As soon as we recognize sin in our life, we need to pray, "Lord, I wandered and I've strayed away from you. Spirit of God, forgive me."

Did you know you can pray to the Holy Spirit? He is a person, and just like you pray to the Father, or to Jesus, you can pray to the Holy Spirit. Tell him, "Holy Spirit, I have offended you. I have grieved you. I have quenched you in my life. Please forgive me. I want you to fill me. I want you to control me. I want to submit to you. Thank you for your forgiveness. Please come into my life and take control of me."

There are Christians who haven't prayed a prayer like that in a long time. It may even be that they have *never* prayed a prayer like that. They are the people of whom Tozer and Torrey spoke when they wrote a century ago that without the Holy Spirit there is no life, no power, no union. There is no vitality and no victory. Jesus came to give life, a full and abundant life.

Jesus said he would send another Comforter like himself. But this Comforter wouldn't live on the outside. He would live inside us. Jesus promised them that when that day came they would know it. When a person is filled with the Holy Spirit of God, he or she knows it! There is no mistaking the filling of the Holy Spirit. It is a truly awesome and powerful force in the life of a believer.

> *Spirit of God, we confess that we haven't always given you full control of our lives. I ask you now to forgive me, to fill me with your power, and to give me the desire to follow wholeheartedly after God. Thank you.*

Application

1. "This abiding in Christ cannot happen without the Holy Spirit." Is the Holy Spirit alive in your life? Do you allow him to control your life and keep you abiding in Christ?
2. "He was a man who was not afraid of the Holy Spirit." Are you ever afraid of the Holy Spirit and the work he might want to do in your life? How can you give up this fear and trust that wherever he guides you, he will go with you?
3. "When people say to me, 'I'm going to pray that the Lord anoints you for this occasion,' I am encouraged, because I really believe in the Holy Spirit's work." For what occasion do you need the Holy Spirit's anointing today?
4. "They believed in the Spirit, but nobody seemed to be experiencing him. Something was wrong." How do you experience the Holy Spirit in your life? What fruit does he enable you to grow that you would not be able to cultivate without him?
5. "We disrupt our connection with the Vine and his life-giving power by the sin we tolerate in our lives. We disconnect ourselves through disobedience." What has disconnected you from the Vine? Ask the Lord to help you live in obedience to him.

CHAPTER 14

BEAR FRUIT

BUT IF YOU MAKE YOURSELVES AT HOME WITH ME AND MY WORDS ARE AT HOME IN YOU, YOU CAN BE SURE THAT WHATEVER YOU ASK WILL BE LISTENED TO AND ACTED UPON. THIS IS HOW MY FATHER SHOWS WHO HE IS—WHEN YOU PRODUCE GRAPES, WHEN YOU MATURE AS MY DISCIPLES.

I'VE LOVED YOU THE WAY MY FATHER HAS LOVED ME. MAKE YOURSELVES AT HOME IN MY LOVE. IF YOU KEEP MY COMMANDS, YOU'LL REMAIN INTIMATELY AT HOME IN MY LOVE. THAT'S WHAT I'VE DONE—KEPT MY FATHER'S COMMANDS AND MADE MYSELF AT HOME IN HIS LOVE.

I'VE TOLD YOU THESE THINGS FOR A PURPOSE: THAT MY JOY MIGHT BE YOUR JOY, AND YOUR JOY WHOLLY MATURE. THIS IS MY COMMAND: LOVE ONE OTHER THE WAY I LOVED YOU.

—JOHN 15:7–12 MSG

L ife in God's vineyard. What's it like for you?

There's a joke that has floated around the Internet for years about Satan and Peter. Satan challenges Peter to a baseball game, and Peter says, "Okay, but you don't have a chance. We have Babe Ruth up here. We have Ty Cobb and Mickey Mantle. You don't have a chance."

Satan laughs and says, "Yeah, that's right. You've got some great people up there, but I've got the umpires."

Is your life in God's vineyard one where Satan has the upper hand? Does he have all the umpires? Is he calling the shots?

One of Murphy's laws says, "If you're feeling good, don't worry. You'll get over it." Maybe some people think of God's vineyard that way, as kind of dull and boring. But Jesus said that life in God's vineyard is going to be a life that is beyond anything that we have ever experienced before!

We've looked at Jesus as our true Vine, and how we need a vital connection to him, as well as to be filled with the Spirit. Now I want to share with you four results of that connection, filling, and abiding relationship. The first result is fruitfulness.

Remaining in Christ Results in Fruitfulness

Jesus told us that when we remain in him and keep his commands, we will bear fruit. The fruit he is talking about is all about his glory, not ours. Jesus says, "You're going to bear much fruit, and the reason you're going to bear fruit is because it will bring glory to God, not glory to yourself." It's sometimes hard to remember that.

One of the works of the Holy Spirit is to give us gifts. When we open our hearts to Jesus, and the Holy Spirit fills us, he gives each of us a special gift. The purpose of those gifts is to bring God glory and to build up the church.

One of the things I have had to realize is that those gifts are there for the building of God's kingdom, not mine. It's so hard for us to grasp that because we live in a very results-oriented society. Everything we do is tied to a certain level of expectation. We look for the results. That's how we measure success. Jesus said that the results that we get from using our gifts are not to bring glory to ourselves. They are to be for the glory of God's Son, Jesus Christ.

Maybe you haven't even identified your gifts yet. You ought to find out what they are. Make a list of the gifts from Scripture (Eph. 4:11–16; 1 Cor. 12; Rom. 12:3–8), and highlight the ones you or your friends identify as strengths for you. Or try asking your pastor, or a mature Christian who knows you well, to help you find your gift(s). When you discover those gifts, understand that we are not to use them in a competitive manner. That goes against our grain. But if God has given us gifts to build his kingdom, which he has, and we use them in a competitive way, we've missed the point.

We can be competitive teachers. We can be competitive administrators. If we have the gift of helps, we can be competitive helpers. If we have the gift of evangelism, we can even be competitive evangelists. It is absurd to think we would ever use God's gifts to compete with one another, but we do. We often compare ourselves to others who have the same gift.

God is very interested in the motivation behind our use of his gifts. He is very interested in the motives that drive our desire to bear much fruit. Is it because we want to bring some accolades to ourselves? Or is it because we really want to help a brother and sister along and to glorify God? God will work to strip away any false spirituality, any ego-based confidence in order to reveal our true motivation for using those gifts. Fruit bearing is for the King. It's not for me, and it's not for you. It's for the King.

Jesus didn't say, "If you remain in me, you'll bear a little fruit." He said the result will be *much* fruit. That fruit is one way to show the validity of our spiritual formation.

What is the fruit of which we speak? He is referring to the character of our souls, the character of our personality, the integrity of our lives, and the evidence of his control.

In Galatians 5:22–26, Paul identified the fruit of the Spirit. He said,

> But the fruit of the Spirit is love, joy, peace, patience, kindness, goodness, faithfulness, gentleness and self-control. Against such things there is no law. Those who belong to Christ Jesus have crucified the sinful nature with its passions and desires. Since we live by the Spirit, let us keep in step with the Spirit. Let us not become conceited, provoking and envying each another.

Notice, Paul didn't say "fruits." He just said "fruit." It's not plural, but singular. It is a singular and total character transformation. We can't pick and choose which little piece of fruit we're going to work on. We can't read the Bible and say, "I'll do this, but not do this." We tend to read and obey the Bible selectively so many times, and we'll often look at the fruit of the Spirit and do the same thing. We'll say, "Oh, I'll work on peace, but I don't really care to work on patience."

Paul taught that the fruit of the Holy Spirit in my life will encompass all the characteristics he lists. A life that bears fruit will develop all these characteristics. We will become more patient. We will turn into gentler people. We will seek to be kinder and to exercise greater self-control. We will display peace, joy, and love.

How can we know if we are connected to the Holy Spirit? Take a look at the characteristics Paul lists in this passage, then ask yourself, "Are these things growing in my life?" If I can't answer the question, all I have to do is ask my wife. She'll tell me. We can put on a show and try to look like super-saints when we show up at church, but the people close to us will know whether or not we are Spirit filled.

A true disciple of Jesus is always becoming more fully a disciple of Jesus. We are always maturing, always growing. Life transformation is not static; it's constantly developing. So we look at our lives, and we ask, "Am I truly yielded to the Spirit of God? Does the Holy Spirit really direct my entire life?" If so, Christ's character and the fruit of the Spirit will be evident in our lives. All the other good fruit we see in the Bible stems from this one question—is our character becoming more like Jesus? When you read the fruit of the Spirit in Galatians, doesn't it sound like Jesus? Take note of all those characteristics, and then go read through the Gospels. You'll see that's how Jesus was. He wants to see those same characteristics become a reality in you and me.

I recently bumped into someone who knew a friend of mine from southern Oregon, a man by the name of Dar. He shared with me how Dar had been influential in his life for many years, as both a coach and a leader in the church. He said, "That man was my rock. I watched his life. I listened to him speak. I never heard anything bad. He never got angry with us as kids. He was always kind. He was always polite. He was always loving."

So I e-mailed Dar the next morning, and I said, "I just met a friend of yours who is now in his forties, and he told me you were the most influential person in his life." Dar had no idea. He had just been allowing the Spirit to control his life, and his life had produced fruit. When the Spirit of God invades our lives and begins that spiritual transformation, it's an exciting thing.

Remaining in Christ Results in Love

The most wonderful words in the world are when someone you care about says, "I love you," or "I will love you forever." But it's even greater when the Spirit of God says the same to you. In the quietness of your soul, when you're alone, when you're weeping by yourself, and you wonder which end is up, the Spirit of God reaches into your soul and mind and whispers to you, "I love you."

It is sad that so many people are emotionally handicapped and cannot express love to others and don't know how to receive love from someone else. Our ability to receive God's love and to return that love to him is one of the most important aspects of our life as a Christian. You will be able to experience that love when your mind can accept by faith that you are, in fact, the apple of God's eye. We must be able to accept by faith a simple statement: "God loves me."

When we submit to the loving care of God and allow him to fill us with his Spirit, we can say, "Lord, I want to know that love. I want to experience that love." With the power of the Spirit in us, he will set us emotionally free. We can then receive God's love and give love back. That's the love Jesus wants us to know. God never intended for us to have a loveless relationship with him.

The fruit of the Spirit is love, joy, peace, patience, kindness, goodness, faithfulness, gentleness, and self-control. But it starts with love—a love that has no beginning and no end. It's not a love that compares with other people and competes with anyone else. It is a love that mirrors his unconditional love for us. Jesus said, "I love my Father. My Father loves me and I love you, and I want you to love me in return."

Remaining in Christ Results in Obedience

We don't really like the word *obedience*. Jesus said, "If you obey my commands, you will remain in my love" (John 15:10). How do we do that? How do we demonstrate our love for him? By our obedience.

The word *obey* refers to a habitual obedience. Jesus said,

"My yoke is easy and my burden is light" (Matt. 11:30). John wrote in 1 John 5:3, "His commands are not burdensome," and they're not heavy to the one who is filled and in vital connection with the Vine, which is Jesus. No, the commands are not difficult for such a person.

Jesus tells us, "Life with me, life in the Spirit, is not some horrible, demanding, and frustrating experience." When we are connected to the Vine, wonderful fruit will supernaturally flow from our lives. We need simply to obey him, to follow the leading of the Spirit, to do what the Lord says to us through his Word. Not in a legalistic manner, not by making up our own rules and regulations, but by pursuing the goal to which Jesus invites us: to become more like him.

I went shopping, and in the store I saw a mother scolding her son. He had done something wrong, and after she finished reprimanding him, he said to her, "I'm sorry." Her immediate response was, "No, you're not."

I thought, *How many times have I said, "I'm sorry," when I didn't really mean it?* Kids say, "I'm sorry," all the time when we threaten them with consequences, but we suspect they're not really sorry. They simply respond to our correction with the most logical thing that could be said at that time—a reply that attempts to avert the dreadful disaster of parental discipline. And their facial expressions often betray their lack of remorse.

After Peter's denial of Jesus in John 18, Jesus comes to Peter after his resurrection. He asks Peter, "Do you love me?" Peter answers, "Yes, Lord." Jesus then repeats the question (21:15–17). We get the impression Peter was just mouthing the words and didn't really mean them.

When Jesus asks him a third time, Peter feels hurt. Peter hadn't been consistently obedient every time, and he knew that Jesus was serious as he gave the instruction "Feed my sheep." Jesus didn't just want Peter to just say, "Yes, Lord, I love you"; he wanted Peter to obey him!

Abiding in Jesus requires obedience. Obedience proves our love for him.

Remaining in Christ Results in Joy

We see the final result of remaining in Christ in John 15:11. Jesus says, "That your joy may be complete."

Do you think God is *happy*? Do you think Jesus ever laughs? I think he does. He told us all these things so that we could have joy. The joy of Jesus should be evident in our own lives. Jesus says to us, "I want you to know my love. My love should remain in you. This is my joy. My joy should remain in you." He earlier said, "Peace I leave with you; my peace I give you" (John 14:27).

For what does the world desperately clamor? It longs for love, joy, and peace. Jesus promises us, "If you remain in me, if you stay connected with me, if the Holy Spirit of God dwells in your life, then you'll have the things everyone is looking for. They will take root at the very core of your being. There will be love, joy, and peace."

Jesus said that when we connect with him—the Vine—life through the Holy Spirit will be a joy.

Henri Nouwen said, "Joy is the experience of knowing that you are unconditionally loved."[1] I wonder how many of us feel true joy in our hearts. Even in the midst of sorrow, can we have joy?

Luke 15 records the famous story of the prodigal son who goes to his dad and says, "Give me everything that's mine." He then rushes off and squanders it. He eventually returns home, and Dad is out by the gate waiting for him. He throws a big party, they kill the fatted calf for dinner, and everyone dances and celebrates.

The older brother is outside finishing up the daily chores, and he hears all the commotion, so he asks a servant, "What's happening?" The servant tells him, "Your brother has come home. Your dad is throwing a party for him." The older brother gets all uptight. He doesn't like it at all.

After all, he had been doing his duty. He is the good son, the hard worker. He has fulfilled his obligations. But now he is a very unhappy son. He was in a kind of bondage. His bondage was the need to live up to other people's expectations. He has always wanted to live up to every expectation others had ever imposed on him.

Perhaps you have lived that way. Maybe you are the oldest son or daughter. You've lived all your life diligently fulfilling the expectations of your parents. Your little brother doesn't give a rip about anybody's expectations, and you look at him and think, *I do all this work, and all this guy does is run around, having the time of his life. And now Dad throws a party for him!*

This older brother was really struggling. He must have at the same time hated and envied his little brother. He hated him because his brother didn't care what other people thought and was getting away with it. He also envied his brother for the fuss others were making over him when he came back.

I often think of that older brother. People talk so often of the Prodigal Son. We all know the Prodigal Son was a pretty lost individual. Many of us have been prodigals. But I find churches in America are filled with even more people like the older brother. The Prodigal Son was lost, but so was the older brother, even though he was a "good boy."

He had done all the right things, but he did not do them out of love. He only worked to please his father because he thought he would eventually get something in return. And when he didn't get what he thought was coming to him, he became resentful. Resentment and joy cannot coexist. Not in the same room, not in the same house, not in the same person. You can't know resentment and joy at the same time.

As I travel and speak in churches, I listen to people who like to talk about the great things they've done. "Oh, I've been

doing this for so many years." "I was a Sunday school teacher."
"I've tithed regularly." But when someone else gets recognition,
they often become resentful.

That's why our motives are so important. Why do we use
our gifts? Our gifts are to bring glory to God, and the moment
we use them to glorify ourselves or to compete with others,
we're on the wrong track. I've spoken many places where I've
shared the platform with other speakers, and I have tried to out-
shine them. There I am, waiting to get up and speak, and I
think, *I'm going to blow these people away. Wait till I get up there.
I'm going to make that other guy look like a lightweight.*

Every time that happens in my life it's obvious that the Spirit
of God is not in control of my life. I am using the gift God gave
me to impress, manipulate, thrill, and to try to direct the attention my way. I know exactly when I'm doing that. Fortunately,
the older I get, the less often it happens. Praise the Lord!

If we have joyless hearts, we need to repent. Jesus said, "My
desire is to put my joy in you." When we remain in him, when
we obey him, when we walk with him, the Holy Spirit fills us,
and our joy is full and complete.

Don't be like the older brother of Luke 15. You don't have
to impress God. You don't have to impress anyone. All we have
to do is enjoy him. If we live trying to impress each other with
what we can do or what we know or how spiritual we are, there
will be no joy. That kind of life is simply madness.

Let's stop trying to impress each other and stop trying to
impress God. Do you really think we can impress God with any-
thing? Give it up. It's not going to happen. We can say, "Oh God,
I've been serving you faithfully for fifty years." And God will say,
"Big deal. Did you serve me for fifty years because you loved me?
Or did you serve me because you expect a reward from me?"

I need the Spirit of God to prune me so I can continue to
grow and bear much fruit for his kingdom and for his glory. But
I've also heard people say, "I'm praying for the Lord to cut this

person off." That's a prayer I don't pray. How am I to know what God is doing in someone's heart? How do I know where they are? How can I know what God is doing to prune and cleanse and deal with that other person? I have no idea. It is judgment and spiritual arrogance to say, "Oh Lord, remove those people." Only God can determine what any person deserves.

We need him to fill us with his Spirit so our lives bring forth fruit and produce the love, obedience, and joy he has for us.

I have a feeling that God intends his vineyard to be the most wonderful place in the universe. I'm just beginning to taste a little bit of that fruit, and it is really wonderful. I pray that wherever you are in your own heart with him, you would say, "Lord, I don't want to be that older brother. I don't want the resentment. I want my life to be full of your joy and your presence."

Life in vital connection with Jesus is different from any earthly pleasure anyone can offer. Life with Jesus is supernatural. May we each experience it daily.

Thank you, Jesus, for giving us your Spirit to fill our lives so that we can bear fruit. Help us to show that fruitfulness through our love and obedience to you and through lives that shine with your joy. Lift us up, we pray.

Application

1. "When we open our hearts to Jesus, and the Holy Spirit fills us, he gives each of us a special gift. The purpose of those gifts is to bring God glory and to build up the church." What gift has the Holy Spirit given you? How do you use it for God's glory?

2. "We can put on a show and try to look like super-saints when we show up at church, but the people close to us will know whether or not we are Spirit filled." Do those closest to you see evidence in you

of a Spirit-filled life? Do they see the fruit of the
Holy Spirit's work in your life on a daily basis?

3. "Our ability to receive God's love and to return that
   love to him is one of the most important aspects of
   our life as a Christian." Do you truly believe and
   accept God's love for you? What makes it hard?

4. "Abiding in Jesus requires obedience. Obedience
   proves our love for him." How do you prove your
   love for Jesus? Is your life one of obedience to his
   Word?

5. "If we live trying to impress each other with what
   we can do or what we know or how spiritual we
   are, there will be no joy." Do you try to use your
   God-given gifts to impress others or even to
   impress God? How can you find joy through
   humility instead?

ABOUT THE AUTHOR AND ETERNITY MINDED MINISTRIES

Over the past two decades across America and in nearly forty countries, Daniel Owens has proclaimed the gospel of Jesus Christ and has communicated the need for personal renewal to hundreds of thousands of people.

Christianity Today profiled Dan as one of fifty "Up and Comers"—one of "the many faithful disciples God has raised up to lead the church into the new millennium." This recognition is the result of his unique ability to adapt his contemporary messages to impact any audience. The British publication *Evangelism Today* says, "Dan Owens has a winsome way with words, and a smile that makes it possible to say almost anything without giving offense."

Dan is also the author of *Sharing Christ When You Feel You Can't; In God We Trust, but Only as a Last Resort; A Faith That Is Real;* and *A Joy That Is Real.* He has helped train thousands of Christians to build bridges to the unchurched world. He is an engaging speaker who is passionate about communicating the need for personal renewal.

Before he founded Eternity Minded Ministries, Dan served with the Luis Palau Evangelistic Association as director of training and an associate evangelist for eleven years.

Dan is a graduate of Christian Heritage College (San Diego, California) and Multnomah Seminary (Portland, Oregon). An approved Staley lecturer for colleges and universities, Dan has been a featured speaker at Alive, Creation Festival, Spirit-Fest Midwest, and other youth events across the country and around the world.

Whether speaking to thousands of teenagers at a rally, college students at a university, adults at a missions conference, or families at a festival, Dan is at home in front of people. Listening to this fun, dynamic, and compelling speaker, audiences are moved to consider *eternity*!

Before crusade and festival meetings, Dan and his associates train Christians in friendship evangelism, counseling, and follow-up. This training increases the effectiveness of the evangelistic outreach and equips church members for ongoing evangelism long after the crusade or festival ends.

Dan and his wife, Debby, have been married for more than twenty-five years. They have three sons: Ben (born in 1982), Jordan (born in 1985), and Taylor (born in 1996).

For more information, contact:
Eternity Minded Ministries
PO Box 502101
San Diego, California 92150
(858) 675–9477
dan@eternityminded.org

FREE ONLINE RESOURCES

Be sure to log onto www.danowens.org today to write a brief letter to Daniel Owens. He would love to hear how this book has helped you enjoy a more authentic faith!

On the www.danowens.org Web site, you will discover a treasure chest of free ministry resources and Eternity Minded Ministries updates. You can also sign up to receive Dan's free ministry newsletter, so you can pray for his ministry, keep in touch, and contact him to speak at your church or conference.

You can find out online if Dan will be speaking in your area, as well as listen to some of his most popular messages and radio programs. You can also request a free CD.

Check it out today!

NOTES

Introduction

1. James Allan Francis, *The Real Jesus and Other Sermons* (Philadelphia: Judson Press, 1926), 123–24.
2. Josephus, *Antiquities of the Jews* (Book XVIII, chapter 3), translated by William Whiston (1737), Public Domain. Full text online at www.ccel.org/j/josephus/works/JOSEPHUS.HTM.
3. Tacitus, *Annals 15.44*, qtd. in Lee Strobel, *The Case for Christ* (Grand Rapids: Zondervan, 1998), 82.
4. Pliny the Younger, *Letters*, trans. William Melmoth, rev. by W. M. L. Hutchinson (Cambridge: Harvard University Press, 1935), vol. II, X:96, cited in Gary R. Habermas, *The Historical Jesus* (Joplin, MO: College Press, 1996), 199.

Chapter 2: The Light of the World

1. Popularly attributed to Helen Keller. Source unknown.

Chapter 3: The Lamb of God

1. Lee Strobel, *The Case for Christ* (Grand Rapids: Zondervan, 1998), 146.
2. Ibid.
3. Ibid., 147.
4. Ibid.
5. Ibid.
6. R. A. Torrey, *Questions Answered* (Chicago: Moody Press, 1909), 9.